Collins

Year 5
Maths & English

Targeted Study
& Practice Book

Jon Goulding and Tom Hall

How to use this book

This Maths and English Study and Practice book contains everything children need for the school year in one book.

A **study page** and a **practice page** for each topic.

'**Remember**' boxes highlight key points

Key words highlighted on each Study page with definitions in the glossary.

Tips give ideas on how to remember key information.

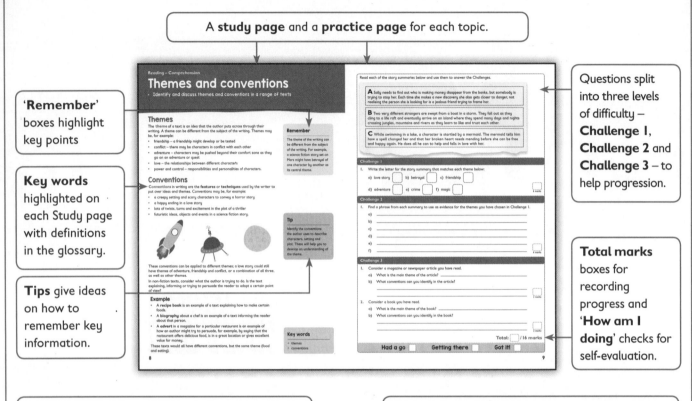

Questions split into three levels of difficulty – **Challenge 1**, **Challenge 2** and **Challenge 3** – to help progression.

Total marks boxes for recording progress and '**How am I doing**' checks for self-evaluation.

Six **Progress tests** included throughout the book for ongoing assessment and monitoring progress.

Mixed questions for maths and English test topics from throughout the book.

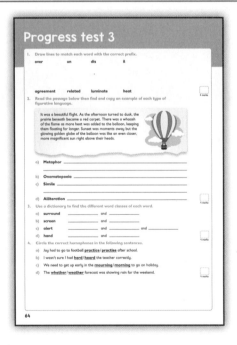

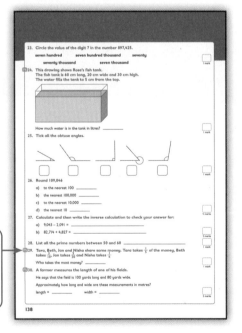

Problem-solving questions identified with a clear symbol.

Answers provided for all the questions.

Contents

ENGLISH

Reading – Word reading

Root words   4

Prefixes and suffixes   6

Reading – Comprehension

Themes and conventions   8

Figurative language   10

Performance and understanding   12

Fact and opinion   14

Retrieving and summarising information   16

Inference and prediction   18

Progress test 1   20

MATHS

Number – Number and place value

Number   24

Place value, Roman numerals and rounding   26

Negative numbers   28

Number – Addition and subtraction

Addition and subtraction   30

Number – Multiplication and division

Special numbers   32

Multiplication and division   34

Written multiplication and division   36

Word problems   38

Progress test 2   40

ENGLISH

Writing – Transcription and spelling

Prefixes and hyphens   44

Suffixes   46

Similar sounding word endings   48

Silent letters   50

Homophones and near-homophones   52

Using a dictionary   54

Writing – Composition

Audience and purpose   56

Organising writing   58

Settings and characters   60

Editing and proofreading   62

Progress test 3   64

MATHS

Number – Fractions including decimals and percentages

Comparing and ordering fractions   68

Adding, subtracting and multiplying fractions   70

Fraction and decimal equivalents 1   72

Fraction and decimal equivalents 2   74

Decimals   76

Percentages   78

Measurement

Converting units of measure   80

Equivalent metric and imperial measures   82

Perimeter, area and volume   84

Measurement word problems   86

Progress test 4   88

ENGLISH

Writing – Vocabulary, grammar and punctuation

Relative clauses   92

Degrees of possibility   94

Verbs and verb tense   96

Cohesion between sentences   98

Cohesion between paragraphs   100

Commas to clarify meaning   102

Parenthesis   104

Progress test 5   106

MATHS

Geometry – Properties of shape

2-D shapes   110

3-D shapes   112

Angles   114

Geometry – Position and direction

Reflection   116

Translation   118

Statistics

Tables and timetables   120

Graphs   122

Progress test 6   124

Mixed questions

English   128

Maths   135

Answers   144

Glossary

Maths   156

English   158

Progress charts   160

Root words

- Apply knowledge of root words
- Recognise how root words can form compound words

What is a root word?

A **root word** is a word that has a clear meaning before any further letters (such as **prefixes** and **suffixes**) are added.

Root words can be used on their own, but prefixes and suffixes cannot.

Adding prefixes and suffixes changes the meaning of the word and can change the **word class**.

Example

The word **disagreement** (a **noun**) has three parts:

Prefix	Root word	Suffix
dis	agree	ment

The root word **agree** is a **verb**.

The root word with the prefix makes **disagree**, which is also a verb.

But the root word with the suffix -**ment** and with the prefix **dis**- make **agreement** and **disagreement**, which are both nouns. The suffix -**ment** changes the word class.

When adding a prefix to a root word, the spelling of the root word does not change. This is not always the case when adding suffixes.

Root words can often have several prefixes and suffixes added to them for use in different ways.

Example

The root word **care**:

*Grandma takes good **care** of me.* ← | **care** is used as a **noun**
*They **care** for their puppy.* ← | **care** is used as a **verb**
*She is a **careful** person.* ← | **-ful** is added and **care** becomes an **adjective**
*Feed the lion **carefully**.* ← | **-ly** is added to **careful** to make an **adverb**

Compound words

Compound words are two or more root words put together to create a new word.

Example

- play + ground = playground
- rain + bow = rainbow
- for + ever + more = forevermore
- white + board = whiteboard
- foot + ball = football
- never + the + less = nevertheless

Two or three root words are put together to make a new word.

Remember

Each word class has a different use: nouns are naming words for people, places and things; adjectives modify nouns and proper nouns (they can also come after the verb 'to be', e.g. Ella *was* tired); adverbs can modify verbs, adjectives, other adverbs or even a whole clause; verbs say what the subject is doing, being or having.

Tip

Look for the root word when reading words. This may help you to read and understand the whole word.

Key words

- root word
- prefix
- suffix
- word class
- noun
- verb
- adjective
- adverb
- compound word

Challenge 1

1. Write the root word for each set of words.

   a) actor, re-enact, acting _____

   b) unlikely, likely, dislike _____

   c) employment, unemployment, employer _____

   d) housing, rehouse, rehousing _____

   e) misread, unread, readable _____

   f) revisit, visitation, visitor _____

   6 marks

Challenge 2

1. Read the passage below. For each underlined word, write the root word in the corresponding box. Use a dictionary to check your spelling.

   Ellie wanted an <u>explanation</u> of the experiment. Her <u>curiosity</u> always made her

   ask lots of questions. <u>Additionally</u>, as she could see, there was <u>insufficient</u> evidence

   to say that the material would become a huge, <u>unrecognisable</u> blob each time.

   5 marks

Challenge 3

1. Add a different root word to the correct prefix or suffix to make each sentence make sense.

   a) The creature crawled _____**ly** up his arm.

   b) A shooting star flashed _____**ly** across the sky.

   c) The shopkeeper was very **un**_____ to make them wait.

   d) She was _____**ful** that they would soon be there.

   e) The writing was **im**_____ to read.

   f) He wanted to **re**_____ the lost pyramid.

   6 marks

2. Add a suffix to the root word to make a new word so that the sentence makes sense. (You might need to change the spelling of the root word before adding the suffix.)

   a) We were very **help**_____ clearing up the mess.

   b) I didn't want to get into an **argue**_____ about it.

   c) The **destruct**_____ was massive.

   3 marks

3. For each of the new words you created in question 2, give the word class.

   a) _____

   b) _____

   c) _____

   3 marks

   Total: ☐ /23 marks

| Had a go ☐ | Getting there ☐ | Got it! ☐ |

5

Prefixes and suffixes

- Apply knowledge of the meaning of prefixes and suffixes
- Recognise how prefixes and suffixes can indicate word class

Prefixes

A **prefix** is a letter or string of letters added to the beginning of a root word. Adding a prefix changes the meaning of the word but does not change the spelling of the root word.

Example

The prefixes **dis-** and **un-** change the root word to mean the **opposite** or 'not':

equal	⇨	**un**equal
(the same)		(not the same)
please	⇨	**dis**please
(make happy)		(make unhappy)

The prefix **mis-** can also give a negative meaning or show that something has been done incorrectly:

| spell | ⇨ | **mis**spell |
| hear | ⇨ | **mis**hear |

Suffixes

A **suffix** is a letter or string of letters added to the end of a root word or a word which already contains a suffix. Adding a suffix sometimes means the spelling at the end of the root word changes a bit.

Example

- care + -ful = careful
- care**ful** + **-ly** = care**fully** ◄ A suffix can be added to another suffix.
- **rely** is a **verb**, e.g. I rely on the van to do my deliveries.
- **reliable** is an **adjective**, e.g. It is a reli**able** van. ◄ Adding a suffix changes the spelling at the end of the root word.

As shown in the example above, adding a suffix can change the meaning of the word.

A suffix can also help to indicate the **word class**.

Suffixes indicating adjectives	Suffixes indicating adverbs	Suffixes indicating nouns
-able, -ible, -ful, -al, -ous	-ly, -fully	-ment, -tion, -sion, -ness, -ance, -ence
Examples: sensible, careful, jealous	Examples: quickly, happily, carefully	Examples: contentment, motion, kindness, attendance

Challenge 1

1. Underline the prefix or suffix in each word below.

   a) mistreat

   b) unhappy

   c) excitement

   d) believable

   e) easiest

   f) illegal

   g) immature

   h) courageous

Challenge 2

1. Insert each version of the word 'explain' in the correct sentence below.

   explain   explanation   explaining   explains   explained   unexplained

   a) Nobody _____ to them how to get there.

   b) She gave an _____ to the class.

   c) The mystery remains _____ to this day.

   d) There was little point _____ as they were not listening.

   e) We tried to _____ what had happened.

   f) The instruction booklet _____ how to make the model.

Challenge 3

1. Using the given root word, add a prefix, suffix or both so that each sentence makes sense. Write the full word in the space given.

   a) He was very _____ teasing his sister.   **kind**

   b) Surely nobody could _____ his clear instructions.   **understand**

   c) The lady _____ gave them directions.   **help**

   d) The _____ car kept breaking down.   **rely**

   e) She was _____ from the race for cheating.   **qualify**

   f) The number ten is _____ by two and five.   **divide**

   g) Layla was _____ with her leaky waterproof.   **impressed**

   h) The jigsaw was _____ as one piece was missing.   **complete**

2. Give the word class of each of these words.

   a) forgiveness _____

   b) personification _____

   c) harmful _____

   d) sadly _____

   e) cautious _____

Total: ☐ /27 marks

Had a go ☐   **Getting there** ☐   **Got it!** ☐

Themes and conventions

- **Identify and discuss themes and conventions in a range of texts**

Themes

The **theme** of a text is an idea that the author puts across through their writing. A theme can be different from the subject of the writing. Themes may be, for example:

- friendship – a friendship might develop or be tested
- conflict – there may be characters in conflict with each other
- adventure – characters may be pushed beyond their comfort zone as they go on an adventure or quest
- love – the relationships between different characters
- power and control – responsibilities and personalities of characters.

Remember

The theme of the writing can be different from the subject of the writing. For example, a science fiction story set on Mars might have betrayal of one character by another as its central theme.

Conventions

Conventions in writing are the **features** or **techniques** used by the writer to put over ideas and themes. Conventions may be, for example:

- a creepy setting and scary characters to convey a horror story
- a happy ending in a love story
- lots of twists, turns and excitement in the plot of a thriller
- futuristic ideas, objects and events in a science fiction story.

Tip

Identify the conventions the author uses to describe characters, setting and plot. These will help you to develop an understanding of the theme.

These conventions can be applied to different themes; a love story could still have themes of adventure, friendship and conflict, or a combination of all three, as well as other themes.

In non-fiction texts, consider what the author is trying to do. Is the text explaining, informing or trying to persuade the reader to adopt a certain point of view?

Example

- A **recipe book** is an example of a text explaining how to make certain foods.
- A **biography** about a chef is an example of a text informing the reader about that person.
- A **advert** in a magazine for a particular restaurant is an example of how an author might try to persuade, for example, by saying that the restaurant offers delicious food, is in a great location or gives excellent value for money.

These texts would all have different conventions, but the same theme (food and eating).

Key words

- themes
- conventions

Read each of the story summaries below and use them to answer the Challenges.

A Sally needs to find out who is making money disappear from the banks, but somebody is trying to stop her. Each time she makes a new discovery she also gets closer to danger, not realising the person she is looking for is a jealous friend trying to frame her.

B Two very different strangers are swept from a boat in a storm. They fall out as they cling to a life raft and eventually arrive on an island where they spend many days and nights crossing jungles, mountains and rivers as they learn to like and trust each other.

C While swimming in a lake, a character is startled by a mermaid. The mermaid tells him how a spell changed her and that her broken heart needs mending before she can be free and happy again. He does all he can to help and falls in love with her.

Challenge 1

1. Write the letter for the story summary that matches each theme below:

   a) love story ☐   b) betrayal ☐   c) friendship ☐

   d) adventure ☐   e) crime ☐   f) magic ☐

   ☐ 6 marks

Challenge 2

1. Find a phrase from each summary to use as evidence for the themes you have chosen in Challenge 1.

   a) _____

   b) _____

   c) _____

   d) _____

   e) _____

   f) _____

   ☐ 6 marks

Challenge 3

1. Consider a magazine or newspaper article you have read.

   a) What is the main theme of the article? _____

   b) What conventions can you identify in the article?

   _____

   _____

   ☐ 2 marks

2. Consider a book you have read.

   a) What is the main theme of the book? _____

   b) What conventions can you identify in the book?

   _____

   _____

   ☐ 2 marks

Total: ☐ / 16 marks

Had a go ☐   **Getting there** ☐   **Got it!** ☐

Figurative language

- Understand and recognise the use of figurative language, including onomatopoeia, alliteration, personification, simile and metaphor

What is figurative language?

Some language is literal – its meaning is obvious and it states exactly what is meant. Literal language is a feature of non-fiction texts.

Figurative language is much more common in fiction and poetry. It is used to help create images in the mind of the reader. There are several different forms of figurative language that appear in texts.

Onomatopoeia

Onomatopoeia is when a word sounds like what it means.

Example

*the **whizz** of fireworks* is a better description than *the noise of fireworks*

*the **hiss** of a snake* sounds much better than *the sound of a snake*

Alliteration

Alliteration is the repeating of sounds in neighbouring or nearby words in a text.

Example

The slowly slithering scary snake describes a snake in an interesting and memorable way because the 's' sound is repeated.

Annie's Amazing Animal Actors Agency. In advertising, an advert can be more memorable for potential customers if alliteration is used. The use of the repeated 'a' sound here makes it memorable.

Personification

Personification is when something is given human or living characteristics.

Example

The fireworks danced in the sky makes the fireworks seem alive.

Similes and metaphors

Similes and metaphors are used to compare things. A **simile** is when two objects are compared using similar characteristics. Similes usually contain the words **as** or **like**. A **metaphor** is used to describe something as if it was something else. Metaphors help the reader imagine what is being described.

Example

*Emmy sat **as** quiet **as** a mouse* is more descriptive than *Emmy sat quietly*.

The school canteen was a zoo.

> A metaphor – the school canteen was clearly not really a zoo but this description helps the reader to understand that the children were a bit like wild animals and maybe even eating like them!

Remember

Authors use figurative language to make their writing more interesting and to help the reader gain a better understanding of characters, settings and events.

> If you say **whizz** and **hiss** out loud, the sounds the words make are like the meanings they describe.

Tip

Look out for examples of figurative language in texts you read. Think about what the author is trying to tell you.

> A simile – the way Emmy was sitting is compared to how quiet a mouse is.

Key words

- figurative language
- onomatopoeia
- alliteration
- personification
- simile
- metaphor

Challenge 1

1. Think about onomatopoeia. Draw lines to match each image to the word which fits best to the related sound.

meow   sizzle   tweet   ding   pop

5 marks

Challenge 2

1. Complete each simile by joining together the correct parts of each sentence.

   a) The clouds were   as fast as a train.

   b) The large man was   as vicious as a tiger.

   c) Nina ran   like balls of cotton wool.

   d) Her temper was   as tall as a tree.

4 marks

2. Complete each sentence with your own words to create a metaphor.

   a) _____ was a burning disc in the blue sky.

   b) The moonlight was _____.

   c) The snow was _____.

3 marks

Challenge 3

1. Read the passage below then write the examples of figurative language in the appropriate spaces below.

   Harry saw and heard amazing things on the safari. Giraffes stood splendidly statuesque, shaded by huge trees. Zebras grazed their way across the wide open grasslands removing the grass like lawnmowers. The boom of distant thunder filled the air and the rain that followed was a wave washing over the dry land.

   a) Onomatopoeia: _____

   b) Simile: _____

   c) Metaphor: _____

   d) Alliteration: _____

4 marks

Total: ☐ / 16 marks

Had a go ☐   Getting there ☐   Got it! ☐

11

Performance and understanding

- Show understanding through tone, volume and intonation when reading aloud

Tone, volume and intonation

- **Tone** is the attitude with which words are meant when said aloud, e.g.
  *"I can't be bothered," said Hetty, **angrily**.*
- **Volume** is how loudly or quietly something is said, e.g.
  *'It's incredible,' **whispered** the scientist.*
- **Intonation** is the rise and fall of the voice when saying something, e.g.
  They could only watch as rain flooded the valley.

  This last sentence could be read in an excited way because the flooding is a welcome or good thing, or in a downhearted way because it is a disaster. Try reading it aloud in an excited way and in a sad way.

Performing poetry

Poetry needs reading with care. It becomes more interesting when you pay attention to how the words should sound when read aloud.

Example

Read this example, then read it again, paying careful attention to the words.

Flashing fields blur by, then,

Details, cows, houses, cars as,

Crawling slowly, this

Giant caterpillar,

In lazy afternoon heat,

Approaches the station and

D r i f t s to a halt.

> **Flashing** and **blur** give an idea of speed. Read this line quickly with excitement.

> Details appear as the train slows down. Start to read slower, and slower (lazily) until you drift to the end of the poem.

Performing playscripts

Playscripts usually give directions for how a character should say the words.

Example

Jack *(horrified)*:	You must be mad! I can't believe you'd even think of it.
Alice *(calmly)*:	It's fine. I have a plan. And I'll train hard. I know it can be done.
Jack *(panicking)*:	I don't know what to say. What about the dangers? What about the sharks? What if you…
Alice: *(pleading)*:	You must trust me Jack. I know what I'm doing.

The words in playscripts give clues about the characters. These clues can then be used to support the performance of playscripts by helping the reader get a better understanding of the characteristics the words represent. For example, from the above script, it can be inferred that Alice is a calm and adventurous character. She's possibly brave too. Jack appears to be more cautious and maybe a bit of a worrier.

Challenge 1

1. Read the playscript below and add a word in each space to describe how the character might be speaking.

    a) **Knight** (_____): I'm not afraid, Dragon. You do not scare me.

    b) **Dragon** (_____): You foolish knight. Now, I will enjoy making you suffer.

    c) **Knight** (_____): Ha, ha. You are old and weak and no match for me.

    d) **Dragon** (_____): I still have enough power for one more atrocity.

    4 marks

2. Consider the words spoken by each of the characters above and write a few words or a sentence to describe each character from the information given.

    a) Knight: _____

    b) Dragon: _____

    2 marks

Challenge 2

Read the poem below. Use this poem to answer Challenge 2 and Challenge 3.

> **Tower block**
> Amazingly tall, standing proud into the sky.
> A concrete monster towering over its surroundings,
> Then the banging, breaking, smashing, shattering,
> Of loud demolition,
> Just rubble now, under a silent cloud of grey dust.

1. a) Which line of the poem do you think should be read in a loud voice?

    _____

    b) Why do you think the tower block is referred to as a 'concrete monster'?

    _____

    _____

    2 marks

Challenge 3

1. Why do you think the poet uses the words 'banging, breaking, smashing, shattering'?

    _____

    _____

    1 mark

2. How do you feel the final line of the poem should be read? Explain your answer, thinking about what emotion the poem is trying to get across.

    _____

    _____

    _____

    1 mark

Total: ☐ / 10 marks

| Had a go ☐ | Getting there ☐ | Got it! ☐ |

Fact and opinion

- Recognise fact and opinion
- Distinguish between statements of fact and opinion

Fact

Statements of **fact** are true. They can be proved with evidence.

Example

- Mike's bike is yellow. ← The evidence to prove this is the bike itself.
- There are 28 children in the class. ← The evidence to prove this is by counting the number of children in the class.

Facts are used to give clear information to the reader.

Opinion

An **opinion** is a viewpoint. A person, or many people, may have one point of view but another person, or many other people, may disagree.

Example

- Mike's bike is a horrible colour. ← Some people will agree; other people will disagree.
- There are too many children in the class.

Opinion gives one possible side to an argument or debate, or is simply shared by an author because they believe it to be relevant.

Recognising fact and opinion

It is important to be able to recognise fact and opinion in texts and spoken language. Distinguishing between the two can help you understand what the author is trying to say. If a text contains opinion, you need to ensure that you do not mistake this for fact.

A good way to check whether something is fact or opinion is to ask whether somebody else could think of something different to say about it. If they can, it is likely to be opinion. Always ask questions about the information presented, and also ask whether there are facts to back up the words written.

Ask whether the point can be proved. If it can, it is likely to be fact.

Example

This text contains a lot of opinion:

> Everyone believes cyclists should be banned from roads. They are dangerous because they are often involved in accidents, and do not obey the rules of the road.

Does 'everyone' really think this?

Is it cyclists who are dangerous?

Is this all cyclists who do not obey road rules?

This text contains fact.

> Cycling can be made safer if everyone takes care. Drivers need to be aware of cyclists, and cyclists must be aware of cars. Wearing a helmet reduces the risk of head injury in the event of a crash.

Everyone using the road should take care.

This is a fact. There is evidence to show this point.

> **Remember**
>
> If you are making a statement about anything from a text, make sure you have evidence to back up your idea.

> **Key words**
>
> - fact
> - opinion

1. Label each statement below as fact (F) or opinion (O).

   a) Custard is very tasty. ☐

   b) Custard is often poured on puddings. ☐

   c) Earth orbits the sun. ☐

   d) The moon is pretty at night. ☐

   e) Ski-jumping is crazy. ☐

   f) Ski-jumping safely requires great skill. ☐

   ☐ 6 marks

Challenge 2

1. Circle the facts and underline the opinions in the text below.

   The English Channel is 34km wide at its narrowest point. People attempt to swim this each year. It is a really silly thing to do. Swimmers need to be brave. There are hazards such as ships to avoid. All swimmers enjoy the experience. To complete the channel swim you need to be a strong swimmer. It is much better to stick to going for walks for your exercise.

   ☐ 8 marks

2. Write a brief explanation of the difference between fact and opinion.

   _____

   _____

   _____

   ☐ 2 marks

Challenge 3

1. a) Write a sentence or two containing a fact about your house or your family.

   _____

   _____

   b) Write a sentence or two containing an opinion about your house or your family.

   _____

   _____

   c) Write a sentence or two containing a fact about something you are interested in.

   _____

   _____

   d) Write a sentence or two containing an opinion about something you are interested in.

   _____

   _____

   ☐ 4 marks

   Total: ☐ /20 marks

   Had a go ☐   **Getting there** ☐   **Got it!** ☐

Retrieving and summarising information

- Know how to retrieve and summarise information from a text

Retrieving information

Being able to **retrieve** information demonstrates your understanding of a text.

Example

The work of Dr Goodlad

Dr Goodlad told the children all about himself and his work with African wildlife. He enjoys eating curry and his favourite colour is blue. For 25 years he has looked after injured giraffes and lions. Many have been orphaned after their parents were killed by poachers.

In the above text, the first sentence is simply an introduction. The second sentence is not at all relevant to what Dr Goodlad does but the third and fourth sentences are.

Example

Dr Martin Luther King was a Christian minister who stood up for the rights of black people in the USA. In the 1950s and 1960s, black people were told to use different public toilets, swimming pools, restaurants and even some shops, to white people. Dr King wanted equal rights for black people and white people, and led demonstrations demanding this. In 1963, a quarter of a million people in Washington DC heard his famous 'I have a dream' speech in which he said that people should not be judged by the colour of their skin.

Who was Martin Luther King?

A Christian minister who stood up for the rights of black people.

What did Martin Luther King want?

Equal rights for black people and white people.

Why did he want this?

Black people did not have the same rights as white people and Martin Luther King believed that people should not be judged by the colour of their skin.

Summarising information

To summarise a text, pick out the main details and key points, writing these in your own words as far as possible.

Example

A summary of the Dr Martin Luther King text above could be:

Dr Martin Luther King was an American Christian minister who fought for black people and white people to have equal rights, believing that nobody should be judged by the colour of their skin.

Summarising information can also help with understanding a text because in order to summarise effectively, the key information must be found and understood.

> **Remember**
>
> When answering questions about a text, read the text and the question carefully before retrieving the information being asked for.

> **Tip**
>
> Underline key words and ideas in a text as you read. This will help you when retrieving and summarising information.

> **Key words**
>
> - retrieving
> - summarising

Read the text below and use it to answer the Challenges.

The road outside the school is so dangerous. There needs to be a much lower speed limit because cars drive far too quickly. A safe place to cross the road is also needed, as well as a proper place to park when we drop-off and pick-up our children. The footpath is narrow and there is no choice but to walk in the road. There have been dozens of near misses and one of these days somebody will get seriously injured, or worse. As parents, we demand that the local council comes to see the situation for itself and puts in place urgent safety measures to protect all pedestrians in the school area.

Challenge 1

1. What is the key word in the first sentence?

_____

1 mark

2. Give three reasons why the road outside the school is considered 'dangerous'.

a) _____

_____

b) _____

_____

c) _____

_____

3 marks

Challenge 2

1. a) How many near misses does the text say have occurred?

_____

b) Give **one** solution that the text suggests will make the situation safer.

_____

_____

2 marks

Challenge 3

1. Write four key phrases from the text.

_____

_____

_____

_____

4 marks

2. Write a summary of the text using no more than two sentences.

_____

_____

_____

2 marks

Total: ____ / 12 marks

Had a go ☐   Getting there ☐   Got it! ☐

Inference and prediction

- Draw inferences from a text
- Predict what might happen next in a text

Inference

Inference means 'reading between the lines' – in other words, deciding what the writer is implying from clues in the text. It can help the reader understand characters and plot, and sometimes the author's point of view.

Example

> Carter gave a big smile and a wink, as the car pulled out of the drive. But inside, his heart felt heavy and he secretly fought back the tears. The adventure had started but how long would it last? Somehow, he had to avoid the Storkman and his assistants.

From this text, you could infer that the smiling, winking character going on an adventure might seem happy, but is feeling sad or worried about something. The final sentence suggests that this something could be the Storkman.

> It had been quite a journey. First, Carter had almost missed his flight because he'd lost his passport in the depths of his backpack. He'd then dropped his tickets and his money under his seat on the plane, and now he could not find the correct piece of paper to hand over for the train ticket. He searched through his belongings, keeping one eye on his surroundings.

More information about Carter can be inferred from this passage. It seems he is not very well-organised with his travel documents – maybe because he is nervous or worried. He's also looking out for something – perhaps the Storkman.

Prediction

Prediction is about considering what might happen in a text from an understanding of what has happened so far. Read the text, then think about what might happen.

Example

> As he now hurried towards the waiting train, a car pulled up. Three thuggish-looking men stepped out and followed Carter, getting closer and closer. Three other thugs approached from the opposite direction. Carter did not notice them and boarded the train. The thugs also boarded.

When predicting events, do not just have a guess or write down what you would like to happen. For example, there is clearly some danger or action coming up for the character, and the story so far seems to indicate some sort of mission. A prediction that Carter has a nice sleep and wakes up at his destination wouldn't really fit with what is known so far.

Remember

Consider how your inferences fit with the text, and which words provide evidence for what you infer.

Remember

The writer **implies** and the reader **infers**.

Tip

Prediction is not just a guess – you must think carefully about the text and how your idea fits with it.

Key words

- inference
- prediction

Challenge 1

1. Read the final text extract on the opposite page. Give two predictions about what might happen next.

_____

_____

_____

_____

2 marks

Challenge 2

1. Underline the sentence in the text below that implies that Alice acted in a mean way.

> Alice watched the others carefully. She did not like the drawing they were creating. Come to think of it, she didn't like them very much either. As Jackson and Kira talked about which colours to use, Alice started to push each crayon down in the pencil pot. The tip of each crayon broke, almost silently and for now unnoticed. She stood up and walked away.

1 mark

2. In the text above, Alice is a new girl, while Jackson and Kira have been friends for a long time. What does this information help you to infer about Alice's feelings?

_____

_____

1 mark

Challenge 3

1. Read the text then answer the questions.

> Narrow shafts of sunlight through two small windows pierced the dusty air of Grandad's attic. Large wooden boxes were piled from the floor to the sloping ceiling. One box contained cuttings from old newspapers; several were filled with maps of strange-sounding places. Another contained what looked like ancient weapons. A final box was empty apart from a brown leather folder with a metal clasp, and an insert with Grandad's name and the words 'Final Plans – Top Secret'.

a) What do the words 'dusty air' help us to infer about the attic?

_____

_____

b) What could be inferred about Grandad from the text above?

_____

_____

c) Predict what might happen in this story.

_____

_____

_____

3 marks

Total: ☐ /7 marks

Had a go ☐   **Getting there** ☐   **Got it!** ☐

Progress test 1

1. Add a prefix or suffix to each underlined root word so that each sentence makes sense.

   a) Everybody was **talk_____** at the same time.

   b) The cat **look_____** at the pigeon.

   c) Somebody had _____**read** the sign.

   d) They **approve_____** the new design for the car.

   e) She was upset because her sister had been _____**kind**.

   5 marks

2. Tick the sentences that are examples of alliteration.

   The towering fence loomed over the garden.

   The graceful dolphins dive deep into the ocean.

   She read the whole book in two hours.

   The wind whistled and wailed through the door.

   The dog hid in the cave on the beach.

   2 marks

3. Complete each simile by joining together the correct parts of each sentence.

   a) Her voice was booming   like a yo-yo.

   b) They were up and down   as quietly as a mouse.

   c) Sam crept along   as loud as thunder.

   d) The beach was   like a small desert.

   4 marks

4. Using the given root word, add a prefix, suffix or both to each sentence so that it makes sense.

   a) The sun kept _____ behind clouds.   **appear**

   b) He wanted a special power to make himself _____.   **visible**

   c) Olly had _____ the task.   **understood**

   d) Suki thought the challenge would be _____.   **possible**

   e) It was the last day of their amazing holiday, _____.   **fortunate**

   5 marks

5. Read the playscript below and add a word in each space to describe how the character is speaking.

   a) Daisy (_____): I'm fed-up being a cow, eating grass all day.

   b) Flossy (_____): Ha ha, you're as bad as the 'udders' with all this moaning.

   c) Daisy (_____): That's an awful joke. Stop talking. Here comes a human.

   3 marks

6. **Read the text then answer the questions.**

Hetty hauled herself over another large boulder. Her legs once again scraped across the rough surface and her knees and hands continued to bleed. She was high up now. A car in the valley below was just a small dot. Looking down made her feel dizzy. Looking up showed her more rocks to get over. She wanted to cry but she knew she must go on.

a) What could be inferred about Hetty from the text above?

_____

b) What evidence from the text supports your inference?

_____

_____

_____

c) What do you predict might happen next in the text?

_____

_____

d) Why did you make this prediction?

_____

_____

4 marks

7. **Add a root word to the correct prefix or suffix to make each sentence make sense.**

a) They **mis**_____ the instructions.

b) The girl _____**ly** helped the old man across the road.

c) Everyone **dis**_____ the people who left litter everywhere.

d) Ellie **un**_____ the present as soon as she got it.

e) We had to be _____**ful** climbing up the cliff face.

f) There was nobody _____**ing** out in the kitchen.

g) They thought it was an **im**_____ task.

h) His handwriting was **il**_____.

8 marks

21

8. **Read the text and answer the questions.**

Last year, I went on holiday with my parents to Orlando. Orlando is in Florida. We went to watch a baseball game, which was amazing. The stadium had a fantastic atmosphere and the Tampa Bay Rays won the game. The weather was perfect and I swam in the pool every day. It was the best holiday ever.

a) Identify two facts in this text.

_____

_____

_____

b) Identify two opinions in this text.

_____

_____

_____

4 marks

9. Write the correct version of **excite** with a prefix and/or suffix in the spaces provided.

exciting   **unexcited**   **excitement**   **excitable**

a) The class were very _____ at Christmas time.

b) They loved watching an _____ film.

c) There was much _____ before Gran arrived.

d) He was very _____ about going shopping.

4 marks

10. Is the following sentence fact or opinion? Explain your answer.

A train journey is very pleasant and relaxing, with interesting views from the windows.

_____

_____

_____

1 mark

11. Add two words to each given word to create examples of alliteration.

a) a _____, _____ smile

b) the _____, _____ cat

c) a _____, _____ house

d) the _____, _____ slug

4 marks

22

12. **Read the poem below:**

Storm at the beach
Fine sand like flour,
Blowing into patterns on the beach.
Wind whipping waves into frenzied foam.
People scurrying to their cars and homes,
Clothes and belongings blowing into the air.
Then heavy rain on windscreens and thunder booming.
Wild rivers flowing into the drains.
And the calm again as the storm drifts away,
And people like quiet mice emerge cautiously from shelter.

a) Give two examples of alliteration from the poem.

_____

_____

2 marks

b) Find and copy the two examples of similes from the poem.

_____

_____

2 marks

c) Find and copy the example of metaphor in the poem.

_____

1 mark

d) What figurative language device is represented by the words 'thunder booming'?

_____

1 mark

e) Explain the difference between how the first seven lines and final two lines of the poem might be read aloud.

_____

_____

_____

1 mark

13. **Give the word class of each of these words.**

a) resentment _____

b) speedily _____

c) unhelpful _____

d) envious _____

e) tension _____

f) confidence _____

6 marks

Total: ☐ /57 marks

Number

- Count forwards and backwards in steps of powers of 10 for any number up to 1,000,000
- Read, write, order and compare numbers up to 1,000,000

Counting

It is possible to count forwards and backwards in steps of **powers of 10**.

Counting in steps of powers of 10, such as 100, 1,000 or 10,000 **adds** or **subtracts** these amounts to the number in each step.

Example

Counting forwards in steps of 100 from 4,872 gives a sequence of:

    4,872   4,972   5,072   5,172   5,272

Counting forwards in steps of 10,000 from 327,247 gives a sequence of:

    327,247   337,247   347,247   357,247   367,247

Counting backwards in steps of 1,000 from 41,184 gives a sequence of:

    41,184   40,184   39,184   38,184   37,184

> **Remember**
>
> Use the place value of the power of 10, e.g. if counting in steps of 10,000, use the tens of thousands column.

Reading and writing numbers

Having commas in bigger numbers helps us to read them.

Example

5,904,027 ← | Use the first comma to read the number of millions and the second comma to read the number of thousands.

This number can be read as:

five <u>million</u>, nine hundred and four <u>thousand</u> and twenty-seven.

When writing numbers, use a comma to separate millions from thousands and a comma to separate thousands from hundreds.

So, four million, five hundred thousand and nine can be written as 4,500,009

> **Remember**
>
> Working from the right, commas identify groups of three digits.

Comparing and ordering numbers

Use place value to compare and order numbers. The greater the place value, the greater the number.

Example

In the number 40,000 there are four tens of thousands.

In the number 37,938 there are only three tens of thousands.

So 40,000 must be the larger number.

Use place value to order numbers.

Example

The numbers 8,924, 7,902, 7,897 and 8,294, starting with the largest, are ordered as follows:

8,924 8,294 7,902 7,897

> **Key words**
>
> - powers of 10
> - addition
> - subtraction

Challenge 1

1. Which two numbers come next in each of these sequences?

   a) 4,654   4,754   4,854   4,954   _____ _____

   b) 37,640   37,630   37,620   37,610   _____ _____

   c) 57,893   67,893   77,893   87,893   _____ _____

   3 marks

2. Circle **fifty thousand, seven hundred and two** written in digits.

   5,702   **50,720**   **5,720**   **50,702**   **500,702**

   1 mark

3. Write these numbers in order starting with the largest.

   5,820   **5,208**   **5,280**   **5,028**   **5,802**

   _____ _____ _____ _____ _____

   1 mark

Challenge 2

1. What is the missing number in each sequence?

   a) 20,927   _____   18,927   17,927   16,927

   b) 132,087   131,087   130,087   _____   128,087

   c) _____   780,952   781,952   782,952   783,952

   3 marks

2. a) Write fifty-one thousand, six hundred and twenty-seven in digits. _____

   b) Write **20,046** in words.

   _____

   2 marks

3. Write these numbers in order starting with the largest.

   32,045   **34,025**   **34,502**   **32,450**   **32,405**

   _____ _____ _____ _____ _____

   1 mark

Challenge 3

1. What are the missing numbers in each sequence?

   a) 802,261   _____   _____   772,261   _____

   b) 367,288   _____   _____   _____   371,288

   c) _____   _____   98,452   _____   100,452

   3 marks

2. This number is written in words, but part of the number is covered.

   four hundred and six ▨▨▨▨▨ **hundred and thirty-six**

   Circle the number that this could **not** be.

   467,236   **460,736**   **446,036**   **406,836**   **406,536**

   1 mark

Total: ☐ / 15 marks

Had a go ☐   **Getting there** ☐   **Got it!** ☐

Place value, Roman numerals and rounding

- Know the value of each digit in a number up to 1,000,000
- Read Roman numerals up to 1,000 and read years as Roman numerals
- Round numbers up to 1,000,000

Place value

Every digit in a number has a value.

Here are column titles showing the value of the digits, for the number 4,721,596

Millions	Hundreds of thousands	Tens of thousands	Thousands	Hundreds	Tens	Ones
4	7	2	1	5	9	6

In the number **700,000** there are five zeros. These zeros are **place holders** and show that the digit 7 is in the hundreds of thousands column, so it has a value of seven hundred thousand or 700,000

> **Remember**
>
> Try to remember the column titles; they will help you to read a number.
> Use commas after the millions column and the thousands column. This will help you to say a number.

Roman numerals

Roman numerals use letters for numbers and are based on the **place value** of a digit in a number.

> **Remember**
>
> These are the Roman numerals:
> I is 1
> V is 5
> X is 10
> C is 100
> L is 50
> D is 500
> M is 1,000

Example

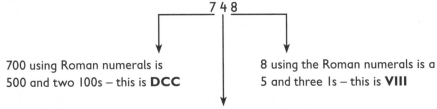

7 4 8

700 using Roman numerals is 500 and two 100s – this is **DCC**

8 using the Roman numerals is a 5 and three 1s – this is **VIII**

40 using Roman numerals is 50 and one 10 less – this is **XL**
(The X is in front of the L)

So, 748 is **DCCXLVIII**

Rounding numbers

Rounding numbers is writing them to the nearest 10, 100, 1,000, 10,000 or 100,000. To round a number, find the digit with that value and check the following digit. If it is 0, 1, 2, 3 or 4 then round down. If it is 5, 6, 7, 8 or 9 then round up.

Example

If 5,648 is rounded to the nearest thousand, look at the thousand numbers below and above the number.

5,648 is nearer to 6,000 than to 5,000, so 5,648 rounded to the nearest thousand is 6,000.

> **Key words**
>
> - place holder
> - place value

Challenge 1

1. In the number **45,732**, what is the value of:

    a) the digit 3? _____   b) the digit 4? _____   c) the digit 5? _____   `3 marks`

2. Find the value of the Roman numerals.

    a) XXXIX _____   b) LXXVII _____   c) CIX _____   `3 marks`

3. Round 45,283

    a) to the nearest 10 _____

    b) to the nearest 1,000 _____

    c) to the nearest 10,000 _____   `3 marks`

Challenge 2

1. Circle the numbers that have a digit 8 with a value of eighty thousand.

    398,026   481,239   1,982,732   81,634   3,803,571   `1 mark`

2. Draw lines to match the Roman numerals to the numbers.

    CXLV   **CCXX**   **XCVI**   **CDIX**   **XXII**

    22   **96**   **145**   **220**   **409**   `1 mark`

3. Round 804,763

    a) to the nearest 100 _____

    b) to the nearest 100,000 _____

    c) to the nearest 10,000 _____   `3 marks`

Challenge 3

PS 1.

| 7 thousands | 5 hundreds of thousands | 5 hundreds | 5 tens of thousands |

Use these four place value cards to make a 6-digit number. _____   `1 mark`

PS 2. These seven letters can be used as Roman numerals:

L, C, I, X, D, X, I

a) Use any four letters once only to make the largest number. _____

b) Use any four letters once only to make the smallest number. _____

c) Use any of the letters once only to make the number closest to CCL. _____   `3 marks`

PS 3. A number rounded to the nearest ten thousand is 830,000

Circle the numbers it could have been.

820,999   835,001   834,867   826,025   `1 mark`

Total: [ ] / 19 marks

Had a go [ ]   **Getting there** [ ]   **Got it!** [ ]

27

Negative numbers

- Understand that negative numbers are numbers less than 0
- Count backwards and forwards across 0
- Solve word problems involving negative numbers

Negative numbers on a number line

Negative numbers are numbers less than 0. They have a 'minus' sign written in front of them to show that they are negative numbers, e.g. -7; this is read as 'minus seven' or 'negative seven'.

Negative numbers can be shown on a number line:

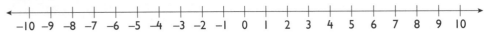

Remember

A number line can be used to count across 0.

Addition and subtraction with negative numbers

Counting forwards is counting to the **right** on the number line.

Example

Counting on 3 is the same as adding 3. Counting on 3 from 6 gives an answer of 9

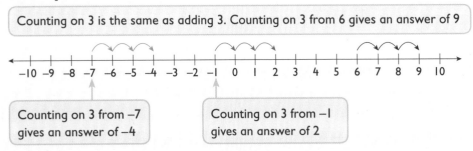

Counting on 3 from −7 gives an answer of −4

Counting on 3 from −1 gives an answer of 2

Remember

The answer to the difference between 5 and -2 is 7 **not** −7

Counting backwards is counting to the **left** on the number line.

Example

Counting back 4 from 10 is the same as subtracting 4. Counting back 4 from 10 gives an answer of 6

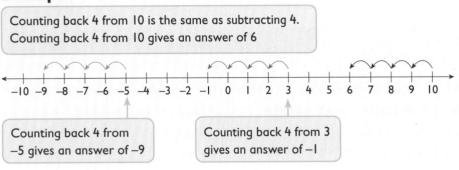

Counting back 4 from −5 gives an answer of −9

Counting back 4 from 3 gives an answer of −1

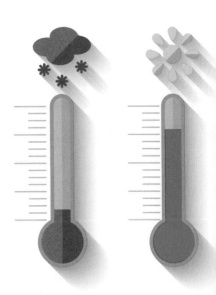

Word problems

Word problems involving negative numbers often use temperature, but could also use things like control buttons in lifts in buildings with floors below ground level.

Example

During the day the temperature outside is 5 °C, but at night it falls by 7 °C. What is the temperature at night?

Using the number line, count back or subtract 7 from 5 to find the temperature at night. The answer is **−2 °C**.

Key word

- negative number

Challenge 1

1. Circle the warmest temperature.

   a) 3 °C   −5 °C   0 °C

   b) −2 °C   0 °C   −1 °C

   c) −7 °C   −3 °C   −10 °C

   3 marks

2. Count back:

   a) 5 from 4 _____   b) 3 from 0 _____   c) 6 from 2 _____

   3 marks

3. Count on:

   a) 6 from −3 _____   b) 7 from −5 _____   c) 8 from −1 _____

   3 marks

Challenge 2

1. Work out the number that is:

   a) 5 greater than −3 _____   b) 3 less than −5 _____

   2 marks

2. Which number comes next in this sequence?

   27   21   15   9   3   ☐

   1 mark

3. What is the difference between these temperatures?

   a) 7 °C and −4 °C _____

   b) 9 °C and −6 °C _____

   c) 2 °C and −12 °C _____

   d) −17 °C and −12 °C _____

   4 marks

Challenge 3

PS 1. a) The temperature inside a classroom is 22 °C. Outside the temperature is −3 °C.

   What is the difference between the two temperatures?

   _____

   b) The temperature in a valley is −2 °C. At the top of a mountain the temperature is −15 °C.

   What is the difference between the two temperatures?

   _____

   2 marks

PS 2. This table shows the temperatures in different cities.

London	Sydney	Berlin	Moscow	Tokyo	Miami
5 °C	16 °C	−4 °C	−11 °C	−6 °C	14 °C

   a) What is the difference in temperature between Berlin and Miami? _____

   b) Which city is 9 °C colder than London? _____

   c) Which two cities have the greatest difference in temperature?

   _____

   d) How many cities are warmer than Berlin? _____

   4 marks

Total: ☐ /22 marks

Had a go ☐   **Getting there** ☐   **Got it!** ☐

29

Addition and subtraction

- Add and subtract numbers mentally
- Use column addition and subtraction for adding large numbers
- Estimate using rounding then check against answers
- Check answers by using the inverse operation

Adding and subtracting mentally

Having a quick recall, for example, 5 + 8 = 13 and 12 − 8 = 4, means calculation will be quicker and more accurate. These facts can be used with larger numbers.

Example

- Using a fact to **add** a 1-digit number to a 2-digit or 3-digit number:

  65 + 8 = 60 + 5 + 8 = 60 + 13 = 73

  243 − 8 = 243 − 3 − 5 = 240 − 5 = 235
- Adding to or **subtracting** a multiple of ten:

  57 + 60 = 50 + 60 + 7 = 117

  80 − 23 = 80 − 20 − 3 = 60 − 3 = 57
- Rounding up or down and adjusting:

  156 + 97 = 156 + 100 − 3 = 253

  374 − 96 = 374 − 100 + 4 = 278
- Finding near doubles:

  68 + 71 = 70 + 70 − 2 + 1 = 139

> **Remember**
>
> Learning addition and subtraction facts by heart will help you to work mentally.

> **Remember**
>
> Make notes or jottings to support mental calculations.

Estimating the answer

Estimating an answer gives an idea of what the answer may be. For example, for the calculation **3,872 − 1,367 =**, rounding the numbers to the nearest thousand gives an estimated answer: 4,000 − 1,000 = 3,000

Column addition and subtraction

Column addition and subtraction is used for **any** calculation that cannot be calculated mentally.

Example

Step 1 – Set out.	Step 2 – Subtract ones.	Step 3 – Subtract tens.	Step 4 – Complete.

3 8 7 2
 − 1 3 6 7
	3 8 $^6\!\!\not7^1$ 2
	 − 1 3 6 7
	      5
		3 8 $^6\!\!\not7$ ¹2
		 − 1 3 6 7
		    0 5
			3 8 $^6\!\!\not7$ ¹2
			 − 1 3 6 7
			 2 5 0 5

	For 2 − 7 =, take a ten from tens column: 12 − 7 = 5	60 − 60 = 0	800 − 300 = 500 3,000 − 1,000 = 2,000

Calculating the inverse

Calculating the **inverse** means using the answer and working back to reach the start number to check.

In the example above, we worked out that 3,872 − 1,367 = 2,505
The inverse (opposite) of subtracting is adding, so:
2,505 + 1,367 = 3,872

> **Key words**
>
> - addition
> - subtraction
> - inverse

Challenge 1

1. a) 39 + 39 = _____ b) 74 − 29 = _____ c) 158 − 7 = _____

2. a) 638 + 757 = _____ b) 769 − 285 = _____ c) 1,734 − 1,094 = _____

3. Calculate and write the inverse calculation for 835 − 429 =

    _____

4. Round the numbers in the questions to the nearest thousand and give the estimated answer.

    a) 6,579 − 1,481 = _____

    b) 9,477 + 6,491 = _____

Challenge 2

1. a) 620 + 33 = _____ b) 800 + 340 = _____

    c) 700 − 4 = _____

2. a) 8,029 − 5,381 = _____ b) 56,439 + 32,884 = _____

    c) 73,989 − 56,472 = _____

3. Calculate and write the inverse calculation for 8,775 − 4,719 =

    _____

4. Round the numbers in the questions to the nearest ten thousand and give the estimated answer.

    a) 68,651 − 23,425 = _____

    b) 74,453 + 40,464 = _____

Challenge 3

1. a) 60,200 + 800 = _____

    b) 70,000 − 900 = _____

    c) 55,100 + 55,200 = _____

2. a) 508,551 − 276,053 = _____

    b) 640,088 + 62,444 = _____

    c) 703,112 − 432 = _____

3. Calculate and write the inverse calculation for:

    a) 308,115 − 7,312 =

    _____

    b) 9,334 + 242,456 =

    _____

4. Round the numbers in the questions to the nearest hundred thousand and give the estimated answer.

    a) 868,651 − 203,884 = _____

    b) 167,321 + 419,777 = _____

Total: [   ] /28 marks

Had a go [   ]   Getting there [   ]   Got it! [   ]

Special numbers

- Identify multiples and factors, including factor pairs, common multiples and common facto
- Identify prime numbers and establish whether a number up to 100 is prime
- Identify prime factors and composite numbers
- Recognise and use square and cube numbers

Multiples and factors

If two whole numbers are multiplied, the answer is a **multiple**:
4 × 5 = 20 (20 is a multiple of 4 and 5).

Other multiples of 4 include 4, 8, 12. Other multiples of 5 include 5, 10, 15.

A **factor** is a number that is multiplied to get another number, so 4 × 5 = 20 (4 and 5 are factors of 20). In this case, 4 and 5 are a **factor pair** of 20.

These arrays show all the factor pairs of 20:

4 × 5   2 × 10   1 × 20

4 is a factor of 20 and it is also a factor of 36, so 4 is a **common factor** of 20 and 36. Other common factors of 24 and 36 are 1, 2, 3, 6, 12.

12 is the largest common factor and so is called the **highest common factor** or **greatest common factor**.

Prime numbers and prime factors

A **prime number** is a number greater than 1 that can only be made by multiplying itself and 1. 19 is a prime number because the only two whole numbers that multiply together to make 19 are 1 and 19.

20 is not a prime number. It is a **composite number** because it can be made by multiplying two whole numbers as well as itself and 1.

Prime factors are factors that are prime numbers, e.g. 3 × 5 = 15, therefore 3 and 5 are factors of 15. As 3 and 5 are also prime numbers, they are called prime factors of 15.

> **Remember**
>
> A prime number can only be divided by itself and 1.

Square and cube numbers

A **square number** is the result of multiplying a number by itself. A **cube number** is the result of multiplying a number by itself twice.

Example

3 × 3 = 9
9 is a square number because units representing 1 can be arranged into a square.

 3 × 3 = 9

3 × 3 can be written as 3^2 ('three squared').

3 × 3 × 3 = 27
27 is a cube number because units representing 1 can be arranged into a cube.

 3 × 3 × 3 = 27

3 × 3 × 3 can be written as 3^3 ('three cubed').

> The digit 2 is the **index**; it tells how many times the number is used in a multiplication.

> Here the index is 3, so the 3 is multiplied three times.

> **Key words**
>
> - multiple
> - factor
> - factor pair
> - common factor
> - prime number
> - composite number
> - prime factor
> - square number
> - cube number
> - index

Challenge 1

1. Here are the first five multiples of 6. Which multiple is missing?

   24   6   12   30   ☐

   1 mark

2. List all the factor pairs of 24 _____ _____ _____ _____

   1 mark

3. Circle three prime numbers in this list: **2   9   11   14   17   20**

   1 mark

4. Write a pair of prime factors of 22 _____

   1 mark

5. a) $5^2 =$ _____   b) $2^3 =$ _____   c) $10^2 =$ _____

   3 marks

Challenge 2

1. Circle three multiples of 7 in this list: **44   54   63   84   97   105**

   1 mark

2. List the factor pairs of 36 _____ _____ _____ _____ _____

   1 mark

3. Apart from 1, write any common factor of 24 and 63   ☐

   1 mark

4. The three prime factors of a number are: **5**, **7** and **9**

   What is the number? _____

   1 mark

5. Which numbers are hidden by the squares?

   a)   ▧$^2 = 64$ _____

   b)   ▧$^3 = 64$ _____

   c)   ▧$^2 = 144$ _____

   3 marks

Challenge 3

1. Find the lowest common multiple of:

   a)   4 and 6   ☐   b)   8 and 12   ☐   c)   6 and 9   ☐

   3 marks

2. Find the highest common factor of:

   a)   12 and 20   ☐   b)   16 and 40   ☐   c)   36 and 45   ☐

   3 marks

3. List the factor pairs of 48 _____ _____ _____ _____ _____

   1 mark

4. List all the prime numbers between 80 and 90 _____

   1 mark

PS 5. a)   Which two square numbers total 100? _____ _____

   b)   Which two square numbers have a difference of 9? _____ _____

   2 marks

Total: ☐ /24 marks

Had a go ☐   **Getting there** ☐   **Got it!** ☐

33

Multiplication and division

- Multiply and divide mentally
- Multiply and divide whole numbers, including those with decimals, by 10, 100 and 1,000

Multiplying and dividing mentally

Quick recall means calculations will be quick and accurate. Knowing one fact means knowing other facts:

If you know that $9 \times 6 = 54$ and $6 \times 9 = 54$, then you know that $54 \div 6 = 9$ and $54 \div 9 = 6$

This can be used for other facts:

$90 \times 6 = 540$, $600 \times 9 = 5,400$, $5,400 \div 9 = 600$, $540 \div 60 = 9$ ...

Example

- Use a fact to multiply multiples of **powers of 10**

  60×40 is the same as $6 \times 10 \times 4 \times 10$ and $6 \times 4 \times 10 \times 10 =$

  > They all equal 2,400

- Partition a 2-digit number and multiply:

  $72 \times 6 = 70 \times 6 + 2 \times 6 = 420 + 12 = 432$

- Use known facts:

  $72 \div 4 = 40 \div 4 + 32 \div 4 = 10 + 8 = 18$

These skills can be extended to larger numbers and to numbers with decimal **notation** such as tenths and hundredths.

Multiplying and dividing by 10, 100 and 1,000

Numbers are based on groups of ten:

- one ten is ten ones
- one hundred is ten tens
- one thousand is ten hundreds.

So, each column to the left is ten times larger than the column to the right. It also means that each column to the right is ten times smaller than the column to the left.

Example

$37 \times 10 = 370$

> The digits 3 and 7 move one place to the left and a place holder 0 is added.

$30.7 \div 100 = 0.307$

> The digits 3, 0 and 7 move two places to the right across the decimal point.

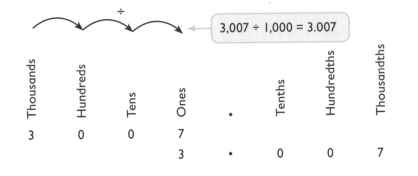

> $3,007 \div 1,000 = 3.007$

Thousands	Hundreds	Tens	Ones	.	Tenths	Hundredths	Thousandths
3	0	0	7				
			3	.	0	0	7

Challenge 1

1. a) $30 \times 7 =$ _____

    b) $2,400 \div 3 =$ _____

2. a) $32 \times 4 =$ _____

    b) $26 \times 5 =$ _____

    c) $85 \div 5 =$ _____

3. a) $57 \times 100 =$ _____

    b) $493 \div 10 =$ _____

    c) $37.6 \times 100 =$ _____

    d) $6.98 \times 10 =$ _____

    e) $71.2 \div 10 =$ _____

2 marks

3 marks

5 marks

Challenge 2

1. a) $90 \times 7 =$ _____

    b) $3,600 \div 90 =$ _____

2. a) $57 \times 4 =$ _____   b) $68 \times 5 =$ _____

    c) $88 \times 3 =$ _____   d) $125 \div 5 =$ _____

    e) $180 \div 6 =$ _____

3. a) $83 \div 100 =$ _____

    b) $508 \div 100 =$ _____

    c) $0.89 \times 100 =$ _____

    d) $804 \div$ _____ $= 0.804$

    e) _____ $\times 100 = 3006$

2 marks

5 marks

5 marks

Challenge 3

1. a) $600 \times$ _____ $= 3,600$

    b) $4,800 \div 600 =$ _____

    c) _____ $\div 90 = 90$

2. a) $4,200 \times 4 =$ _____   b) $280 \times 5 =$ _____

    c) $507 \times 6 =$ _____   d) $2,500 \div$ _____ $= 500$

    e) $7,200 \div 6 =$ _____

3. a) $31.2 \times$ _____ $= 3,120$

    b) $493 \div$ _____ $= 0.493$

    c) $0.087 \times$ _____ $= 87$

    d) $9.05 \times$ _____ $= 905$

    e) $7.8 \div$ _____ $= 0.078$

3 marks

5 marks

5 marks

Total: [ ] /35 marks

Had a go [ ]   **Getting there** [ ]   **Got it!** [ ]

35

Written multiplication and division

- Multiply numbers with up to four digits by one- and two-digit numbers, including using long multiplication
- Divide numbers with up to four digits by one-digit numbers using short division

Multiplication by one-digit numbers

Column **multiplication** is a way of setting out a written multiplication.

Example

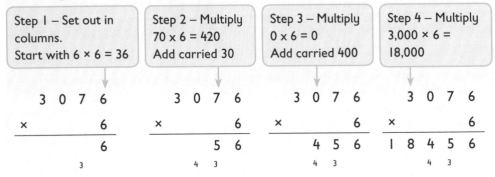

| Step 1 – Set out in columns. Start with 6 × 6 = 36 | Step 2 – Multiply 70 × 6 = 420 Add carried 30 | Step 3 – Multiply 0 × 6 = 0 Add carried 400 | Step 4 – Multiply 3,000 × 6 = 18,000 |

> **Remember**
>
> Always start multiplying with the ones column and work to the left.

> **Tip**
>
> Take care when carrying figures when multiplying so they are not added a second time in the addition.

Long multiplication is a way of setting out a written multiplication.

Example

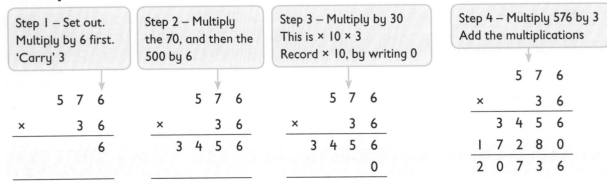

| Step 1 – Set out. Multiply by 6 first. 'Carry' 3 | Step 2 – Multiply the 70, and then the 500 by 6 | Step 3 – Multiply by 30 This is × 10 × 3 Record × 10, by writing 0 | Step 4 – Multiply 576 by 3 Add the multiplications |

Short division

Short division is a method of written **division** with remainders worked out mentally. Keep the answers to each division in the correct column.

Example

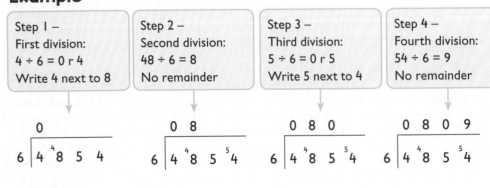

| Step 1 – First division: 4 ÷ 6 = 0 r 4 Write 4 next to 8 | Step 2 – Second division: 48 ÷ 6 = 8 No remainder | Step 3 – Third division: 5 ÷ 6 = 0 r 5 Write 5 next to 4 | Step 4 – Fourth division: 54 ÷ 6 = 9 No remainder |

Answer: **809**

> **Key words**
>
> - multiplication
> - long multiplication
> - short division
> - division

Challenge 1

1. a) 842 × 4 = _____   b) 237 × 6 = _____

    c) 625 × 5 = _____   d) 498 × 4 = _____

    e) 608 × 7 = _____

2. Calculate using long multiplication:

    a) 48 × 24 = _____   b) 65 × 32 = _____

    c) 56 × 16 = _____   d) 63 × 36 = _____

    e) 68 × 84 = _____

3. a) 744 ÷ 3 = _____   b) 525 ÷ 5 = _____

    c) 664 ÷ 8 = _____   d) 492 ÷ 6 = _____

    e) 392 ÷ 7 = _____

Challenge 2

1. a) 2,395 × 4 = _____   b) 2,607 × 5 = _____

    c) 4,527 × 6 = _____   d) 4,562 × 8 = _____

    e) 2,836 × 9 = _____

2. Calculate using long multiplication:

    a) 772 × 26 = _____   b) 495 × 35 = _____

    c) 784 × 43 = _____   d) 801 × 57 = _____

    e) 651 × 64 = _____

3. a) 6,844 ÷ 4 = _____   b) 7,025 ÷ 5 = _____

    c) 5,376 ÷ 7 = _____   d) 5,064 ÷ 8 = _____

    e) 6,174 ÷ 9 = _____

Challenge 3

1. a) 6,567 × 6 = _____   b) 3,754 × 8 = _____

    c) 5,467 × 9 = _____   d) _____ × 6 = 7,488

    e) _____ × 7 = 6,888

2. Calculate using long multiplication:

    a) 6,725 × 64 = _____   b) 6,731 × 25 = _____

    c) 7,273 × 48 = _____

    d) Which two numbers that are the same multiply to give 2,916? _____

3. a) 9,840 ÷ 4 = _____   b) 9,016 ÷ 7 = _____

    c) 5,598 ÷ 9 = _____   d) _____ ÷ 9 = 345

    e) 8,973 ÷ _____ = 9

Total: [ ] /44 marks

Had a go [ ]   **Getting there** [ ]   **Got it!** [ ]

Word problems

- Solve problems using the four rules of arithmetic, including understanding the equals sign
- Solve problems using multiplication and division, factors, multiples, squares, cubes and rates.

Tip

The skills for solving addition and subtraction word problems will apply here too.

Problems using the equals sign

The equals sign is like a balance: whatever is on one side of the equals sign must be the same as what is on the other.

Example

Ben has some football cards in an album. There are 24 pages with 5 coloured cards on a page. He also has the same number of black and white cards with 6 cards on a page. How many pages of black and white cards are there?

$24 × 5 = 120$ ⟵   Pages × Coloured cards per page

$120 ÷ 6 = 20$ ⟵   Total cards ÷ Cards per page

Answer: There are **20** pages with black and white cards.

Problems using factors and multiples

Factors and **multiples** can be used to solve problems.

Example

Abby finds some insects and each has 6 legs. She finds some spiders and each has 8 legs. Altogether there are 62 legs in Abby's collection. How many insects and spiders could be in Abby's collection?

Multiples of 6: 6, 12, 18, 24, 30, 36, 42, 48, 54, 60   Multiples of 8: 8, 16, 24, 32, 40, 48, 56, 64 ⟵ Look for two numbers that total 62

Answer: Either **5 insects + 4 spiders** or **9 insects + 1 spider**

Problems using squares and cubes

Square numbers and **cube numbers** can also be used to solve problems.

Example

Javid's age is a square number. In two years' time it will be a cube number. How old is Javid now?

Square numbers: 1, 4, 9, 16, 25, 36, 49, 64, 81, 100   Cube numbers: 1, 8, 27, 64, 125 ⟵ Look for a cube number 2 more than a square number.

Answer: Javid is **25 years old**

Problems using scales and rates

A **scale** is used in maps and model-making where one unit of measurement represents another. A **rate** is a comparison of related measurements or amounts.

Every 1 cm on the model represents 500 cm on the real ship.

Example

A model ship is built to a scale of 1 : 500 (1 to 500). If the model is 40 cm long, what is the real-life measurement of the ship in metres?

If the model is 40 cm, this means the ratio (scale) is 40 : ?

Convert cm to m by dividing by 100, so $20,000 ÷ 100 = 200$

$$× 40$$
$$1 : 500 \quad\quad 40 : 20,000 \quad\quad 500 × 40 = 20,000 \text{ cm}$$
$$× 40$$

Answer: The actual ship is **200 m** long.

This uses the rate of 2 pitches painted in every 95 minutes.

Example

Jenny paints the lines on football pitches. It takes her 95 minutes to paint the lines on 2 pitches. How long will it take her to paint the lines on 8 pitches?

$8 ÷ 2 = 4$ ⟵   Number of pitches ÷ Number of pitches painted in 95 mins

$95 × 4 = 380$ ⟵

Answer: 380 minutes = **6 hours 20 minutes**

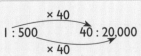
95 mins × Number of groups of 2 pitches

Key words

- factor
- multiple
- square number
- cube number
- scale
- rate

Challenge 1

PS **1.** Tins of beans are delivered in trays of 48 cans. A shop receives a delivery of 18 trays.

How many tins are delivered? _____

[ ] 1 mark

PS **2.** A group is performing six sell-out shows at a theatre. 9,888 tickets have been sold altogether.

How many tickets have been sold for one show? _____

[ ] 1 mark

PS **3.** Find the missing number:

$436 \times 7 =$ _____ $\div 4$

[ ] 1 mark

PS **4.** Mohan's age is a square number and his uncle's age is a cube number. Mohan's uncle is three times older.

How old is Mohan? _____

[ ] 1 mark

Challenge 2

PS **1.** A stand at a football ground has rows of 187 seats. There are 28 rows.

How many seats are in the stand? _____

[ ] 1 mark

PS **2.** 3,600 apples are packed into 8 crates. A crate is delivered to a shop and the apples are packed into bags of 6 apples.

How many bags of 6 are there from one crate? _____

[ ] 1 mark

PS **3.** Ben gives the books he has read either 4 stars or 5 stars according to how much he enjoyed them. He has awarded a total of 53 stars.

How many books could have been given 4 stars and how many 5 stars? Give one possibility.

_____

[ ] 1 mark

PS **4.** Holly can run 1,500 m in $5\frac{1}{2}$ minutes. Penny can run 1,000 m in 4 minutes. If they can both keep running at the same pace, how much quicker will Holly run 6,000 m than Penny?

_____

[ ] 1 mark

Challenge 3

PS **1.** A cruise ship has space for 3,278 passengers. The cruise company owns 15 identical ships.

How many passengers could be accommodated on its 15 ships?

_____

[ ] 1 mark

PS **2.** The hens on a chicken farm lay 7,386 eggs. The eggs are packed into boxes of 6 or 8 eggs.

There are 825 boxes of 6 eggs and the rest are packed into boxes of 8

How many boxes of 8 are filled? _____

[ ] 1 mark

PS **3.** Mia has £75 in seven notes. She has £5, £10 and £20 notes.

How many of each note does Mia have? Give one possibility.

_____

[ ] 1 mark

PS **4.** Zak and Sam go walking. They use different maps. Zak's map has a scale of 2 cm to 5 km and Sam's map has a scale of 1 cm to 10 km. Zak's route is 20 cm on the map and Sam's route is 4 cm on his map.

How much longer is Zak's actual route than Sam's route? _____

[ ] 1 mark

Total: [ ] / 12 marks

Had a go [ ]   **Getting there** [ ]   **Got it!** [ ]

Progress test 2

1. **Fill in the missing numbers in these sequences.**

   a) 32,830   31,830   30,830   _____   28,830

   b) 707,882   708,882   _____   710,882   711,882

   2 marks

2. a) Circle the number with five thousand:

      359,298   43,590   2,598   265,024   51,876

   b) Circle the number with seven tens of thousands:

      87,920   257,619   378,209   7,471   741,876

   2 marks

3. a) 4,287 + 3,925 = _____   b) 8,042 – 2,951 = _____

   2 marks

4. a) 7^2 = _____   b) 4^3 = _____

   2 marks

5. a) 626 + 50 = _____   b) 800 – 12 = _____

   c) 316 – 98 = _____   d) 577 + 97 = _____

   4 marks

6. **Write these numbers in order, starting with the smallest.**

   34,675   34,756   35,476   34,765   35,674

   _____   _____   _____   _____   _____

   1 mark

PS 7. A rugby ground can hold 21,955 spectators. There are four sides to the ground. Three of the sides hold 3,835, 4,087 and 7,266.

   How many spectators can the fourth side hold?

   _____

   1 mark

8. Harry must calculate 5,933 + 3,473 + 4,419 =

   He estimates the answer by rounding each number to the nearest thousand.

   What is Harry's estimated answer?

   _____

   1 mark

9. **List all the factor pairs of 48.**

   _____

   1 mark

10. **Round these numbers to the nearest thousand.**

    a) 2,833   _____   b) 60,045   _____

    c) 183,099   _____   d) 909,909   _____

    4 marks

PS 11. The temperature at 8:00 a.m. was –2 °C. By 2:00 p.m. there had been an increase of 9 °C but by 8:00 p.m. the temperature had fallen by 12 °C.

    What is the temperature at 8:00 p.m.?

    _____

    1 mark

12. **Which numbers are represented by these Roman numerals?**

    a) XXXIX = _____   b) LXXIX = _____

    c) XCIV = _____   d) XLVIII = _____

    4 marks

13. Calculate the missing numbers.

a) 6,390 − _____ = 2,088

b) 5,967 + _____ = 8,562

c) _____ − 5,924 = 3,587

3 marks

14. Write these numbers using digits:

a) fifty thousand and sixty-seven _____

b) two hundred and four thousand, five hundred and six _____

c) nine hundred and twenty thousand and seventy-eight _____

3 marks

PS 15. Manisha has some place value cards.

3 tens of thousands	9 ones	5 thousands
2 thousands	6 tens	6 thousands
7 hundreds	8 ones	4 hundreds

What is the largest number that Manisha can make? _____

1 mark

16. a) 70 × 40 = _____   b) 63 × 6 = _____   c) 91 ÷ 7 = _____

3 marks

PS 17. List all the prime numbers between 30 and 40 _____

1 mark

18. One year a survey estimates there are 7,175 peacocks living on an island. The following year, the estimated population has fallen by 350.

What is the new estimated population?

_____

1 mark

19. Which year is represented by the Roman numerals: MMXIV?

_____

1 mark

PS 20. Ali calculates 5,474 ÷ 7 = 782

Write the inverse calculation that Ali could use to check his answer.

_____

1 mark

PS 21. Melanie makes necklaces with beads. She buys 3 jars with 750 beads in each. She uses 8 beads for each bracelet.

How many bracelets can Melanie make?

_____

1 mark

22. a) 6,935 × 6 = _____   b) 7,826 ÷ 7 = _____   c) 5,130 ÷ 9 = _____

    d) 9,053 × 8 = _____   e) 8,004 ÷ 6 = _____

5 marks

PS 23. This is a panel in a lift showing all the floors in an office building.

Lift	
Floor 6 ●	Floor 5 ●
Floor 4 ●	Floor 3 ●
Floor 2 ●	Floor 1 ●
Floor 0 ●	Floor −1 ●
Floor −2 ●	Floor −3 ●

Milly arrives at the ground floor (Floor 0).

She goes down two floors for a meeting.

Next, she goes up 7 floors to see her manager.

On which floor is her manager? _____

1 mark

24. Round 528,910 to:

    a)   the nearest hundred thousand _____   b)   the nearest hundred _____

    c)   the nearest thousand _____

3 marks

PS 25. What are the two missing numbers in each of these calculations?

a)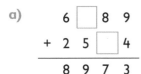

```
    6 □ 8 9
  + 2 5 □ 4
  ─────────
    8 9 7 3
```

b)
```
    7 □ 8 3
  − 2 4 7 □
  ─────────
    4 6 0 4
```

2 marks

PS 26. At the beginning of March, a shop has 5,245 comics on display. A further 2,789 comics are held in the stockroom. The shop owner buys 750 more comics. Over the month, 2,144 comics are sold online and 378 are sold in the shop.

How many comics does the shop owner have at the end of March?

_____

1 mark

PS 27. The population of five towns are listed in a table.

Town	Ashton	Bilton	Cardbury	Dalfield	Emthan
Population	102,864	102,188	101,974	103,092	98,572

Which town has the largest population?

_____

1 mark

28. a)   Which number is the lowest common multiple of 3 and 4? _____

    b)   Which number is the highest common factor of 36 and 48? _____

2 marks

PS 29. Find the missing number:

    6,282 ÷ 6 = _____ ÷ 9

1 mark

42

PS 30. The table shows the temperatures through one day.

Time	4:00 a.m.	8:00 a.m.	12:00 p.m.	4:00 p.m.	8:00 p.m.
Temperature	−6 °C	1 °C	4 °C	−1 °C	−3 °C

How many more degrees colder is it at 8:00 p.m. than at 12:00 p.m.? _____

1 mark

PS 31. Maggie completes a calculation. She starts with 125,000 and subtracts thirty thousand, and then subtracts eight thousand.

What is the answer to Maggie's calculation? _____

1 mark

32. a)   34,900 +199 = _____   b)   4,999 × 5 = _____   c)   40,000 ÷ 8 = _____

3 marks

PS 33. A machine produces 1,875 spoons in an hour. The spoons are packed into boxes of 6.

How many boxes will be filled in 8 hours? _____

1 mark

PS 34. The number of fans at a football match is 28,162. A newspaper reports the number rounded to the nearest 100.

What is the number of fans reported by the newspaper?

_____

1 mark

35. a)   6 − 10 = _____   b)   −6 − 5 = _____   c)   5 − 8 + 2 = _____

3 marks

PS 36. Yasmin plays a computer game collecting eight bags of gold. Each bag of gold is worth the same number of points. The eight bags of gold are worth 10,000 points altogether. Yasmin has collected five bags of gold.

How many points does Yasmin have?

_____

1 mark

PS 37. Fill in the two missing numbers in each of these calculations:

a)
```
      6 □ 7 □
    ×       4
   ──────────
    2 6 3 1 2
```

b)
```
        8 7 9
      ┌─────────
    6 │ 5 ⁵ □ ⁴ 7 ⁵ □
```

2 marks

PS 38. Ravi has a secret number. He multiplies the number by 7 and then divides the answer by 8

The answer is 1,176

What is Ravi's secret number? _____

1 mark

PS 39. The scale used to draw the plans for a new kitchen is 1 cm to 0.4 m.

On the plan, the kitchen is 15 cm long and 9 cm wide.

What is the length and width of the kitchen in real life?

length = _____   width = _____

2 marks

40. What are the missing numbers?

a)   5.06 ÷ _____ = 0.506   b)   9.43 × _____ = 943

2 marks

Total: [ ] /74 marks

Prefixes and hyphens

- Use prefixes correctly
- Use the hyphen correctly

Prefixes

A **prefix** changes the meaning of the **root word** it is added to.

Example

effective ⇨ **in**effective

possible ⇨ **im**possible

As with the examples above, many prefixes give a word its opposite meaning but this is not always the case.

Example

market ⇨ **super**market

marine ⇨ **sub**marine

In the examples directly above, the prefix just creates a word with a different meaning (rather than an opposite meaning).

Verb prefixes

Adding a prefix to a **verb** can change the meaning in different ways.

Example

mis- = wrong, e.g.   read ⇨ **mis**read
I misread the road sign.

re- = again, e.g.   move ⇨ **re**move
They had to remove the poster.

dis- = not, e.g.   appear ⇨ **dis**appear
I just wanted to disappear.

de- = opposite, e.g.   compose ⇨ **de**compose
The leaves decompose in the soil.

over- = too much, e.g. paid ⇨ **over**paid
They overpaid for their tickets.

> Note that these prefixes can also be added to nouns, e.g. **mis**understanding, **re**adjustment, **dis**appearance, **de**activation, **over**payment.

Using the hyphen

Sometimes you need to use a **hyphen** when adding a prefix to a root word.

Example

- After the prefix **ex**, e.g. **ex**-manager, **ex**-dancer, **ex**-wife.
- After the prefix **self**, e.g. **self**-respect, **self**-confidence.
- To separate two identical letters, e.g. **re**-enter, **co**-operate.
  (But, note that words with the **co-** prefix are also often written without a hyphen).
- To avoid confusion, e.g. **re**-cover (cover something again) compared to recover (get better from something).

Remember

Prefixes are not only added to root words. They can be added to words that already have a suffix such as respect**ful**, which becomes **dis**respect**ful**.

Tip

Make sure you are confident at spelling and understanding the root word before adding the prefix.

Key words

- prefix
- root word
- verb
- hyphen

1. Draw lines to match each word with the correct prefix.

| practical | sane | usual | appear | legal |

| un | il | im | in | re |

5 marks

2. Write a further example word for each prefix given above.

a) un_____

b) il_____

c) im _____

d) in_____

e) re_____

5 marks

1. Add a prefix to each underlined word so that each sentence makes sense.

a) The decision to cancel sports day proved to be very _____popular.

b) The bad weather caused them to _____arrange their sports day.

c) There was a complete _____regard for children as the swings were taken away.

d) A _____understanding meant that the sports pitches were not available.

4 marks

2. Add a word to each prefix to ensure each sentence makes sense.

a) The television wasn't working so she tried to **re**_____ it.

b) His handwriting was so bad it was **il**_____.

c) The young man's tantrums and moodiness made him seem very **im**_____.

3 marks

1. Write a sentence that includes the given root word with the addition of a prefix.

a) heard

_____

_____

b) heat

_____

_____

c) treat

_____

_____

d) arrange

_____

_____

4 marks

Total: [ ] /21 marks

Had a go [ ]   **Getting there** [ ]   **Got it!** [ ]

Suffixes

- Convert nouns and adjectives into verbs using suffixes

Changing word class

Adding a **suffix** (a letter or group of letters) to the end of a word can change the word class of the word. For example, the suffixes **-en**, **-ise**, **-ify** and **-ate** change **nouns** and **adjectives** into **verbs**.

Example

Adding -en

straight (adjective)   *She has very **straight** hair.*

⇩

straight**en** (verb)   *She likes to **straighten** her curly hair.*

-en is usually added with no change to the root word, but an example of an exception to this rule is:

flat ⇨ fla**tt**en ⟵ | An extra **t** is added.

Adding -ise

advert (noun)   *He created an **advert** for the shop.*

⇩

advert**ise** (verb)   *The shop could now **advertise** its products.*

-ise is usually added with no change to the root word, but examples of exceptions to this rule are:

fertil**e** ⇨ fertil**ise** ⟵ | The **e** is removed.

apolog**y** ⇨ apolog**ise** ⟵ | The **y** is removed.

Adding -ify

solid (noun)   *Metal is usually a **solid**.*

⇩

solid**ify** (verb)   *When melted, metal will cool and **solidify**.*

-ify is often added with no change to the root word, but examples of exceptions to this rule are:

not**e** ⇨ not**ify** ⟵ | The **e** is removed.

horr**or** ⇨ horr**ify** ⟵ | The **or** is removed.

Adding -ate

alien (used as an adjective)   *Her old friends now seemed quite **alien** to her.*

⇩

alien**ate** (verb)   *She will **alienate** her friends if she isn't careful.*

In some cases, **-ate** is just added to the root word, but examples of exceptions to this rule are:

medic**al** ⇨ medic**ate** ⟵ | The **al** is removed.

poll**e**n ⇨ poll**i**n**ate** ⟵ | The **e** is changed to **i**.

captiv**e** ⇨ captiv**ate** ⟵ | The **e** is removed.

Remember

Adding a suffix to a word may change the word class, e.g. help (verb) + -ful (suffix) = helpful (adjective).

Tip

Always be careful of exceptions to the general rule when adding suffixes.

Key words

- suffix
- noun
- adjective
- verb

Challenge 1

1. Change each word below into a verb by adding **-ise**, **-ate**, **-en** or **-ify**.

   a) length_____   final_____   solid _____

   b) test_____   valid_____   visual_____

   c) special_____   soft_____   advert_____

   d) tight_____   elastic_____   hard_____

Challenge 2

1. Look at each pair of words below. These are exceptions to the spelling rule for the given suffix. Explain what changes have been made to each in order to add the suffix and change it into a verb.

   a) fat (adjective) ⇨ fatten (verb)

   _____

   b) sympathy (noun) ⇨ sympathise (verb)

   _____

   c) terror (noun) ⇨ terrify (verb)

   _____

2. Use each of the above **verbs** in a sentence.

   a) _____

   _____

   b) _____

   _____

   c) _____

   _____

Challenge 3

1. a) Explain what happens to words that end in **e** (such as 'fortune' and 'pure') when adding the suffixes **-ate** and **-ify**.

   _____

   _____

   _____

   b) Give an example of each of the words with their suffixes in a sentence.

   _____

   _____

   _____

   _____

Total: [____] /21 marks

Had a go [ ]   **Getting there** [ ]   **Got it!** [ ]

Similar sounding word endings

- Distinguish between word endings that are often confused

Word endings -cious, -tious and -xious

The **word endings -cious** and **-tious** are often confused in spelling. This is because they sound very similar when said out loud.

A general rule is that if there is an obvious root word ending in **-ce**, then the **-cious** suffix is usually used.

Example

gra**ce** ⇨ gra**cious**

*The team was very **gracious** in defeat, applauding the opposition.*

vi**ce** ⇨ vi**cious**

*The cat became terribly **vicious** if it saw another cat.*

fier**ce** ⇨ fero**cious**

*The creature was **ferocious**.*

For help with many of these spellings, particularly **-tious**, it is worth looking at other words in the same **word family**.

Example

infec**t** ⇨ infec**tion** ⇨ infec**tious**

*After being taken ill, the doctor said she would be **infectious** for 48 hours.*

cau**tion** ⇨ cau**tious**

*I find it is important to be **cautious** if there is a dangerous situation.*

ambi**tion** ⇨ ambi**tious**

*Their design for a working cardboard space rocket was rather **ambitious**.*

Other words in the word family have a **t**, so it is likely that the -tious ending will be used.

There are of course exceptions. For example, an**xious** has the same sound but is spelt with **-xious**.

Word endings -cial and -tial

The endings **-cial** and **-tial** are also easily confused because they sound the same when said out loud.

A general rule to remember is that **-cial** is a more common spelling after a vowel and **-tial** is more common after a consonant.

Example

-cial	-tial
offi**cial**	par**tial**
artifi**cial**	confiden**tial**
ra**cial**	essen**tial**

Be careful though – again there are exceptions. For example, ini**tial** and finan**cial**.

CAUTION

Remember

If you are unsure of the correct spelling of a word ending, refer to a dictionary for help.

Key words

- word ending
- word family

Challenge 1

1. Write the root word for each of the words below.

   a) spacious _____

   b) infectious _____

   c) official _____

   d) partial _____

   e) racial _____

   5 marks

Challenge 2

1. Complete each sentence with the correct word from the list below.

   confidential   **cautious**   **essential**   **fictitious**

   a) They needed to be _____ .

   b) Their help was _____ .

   c) It was a _____ story.

   d) The letter was _____ .

   4 marks

2. Write the correct spelling for the underlined word in each sentence. Use a dictionary to help you, if you are unsure.

   a) The meal was **delitious**. _____

   b) The letter was written on **offitial** paper. _____

   c) Winning the game was **essencial** for the team. _____

   d) The new playground rules were highly **contencious**. _____

   4 marks

Challenge 3

1. Use the correct **-cious**, **-tious** or **-cial** ending to rewrite each word as an adjective. Use a dictionary to help you if you are unsure.

   a) suspicion _____

   b) nutrition _____

   c) malice _____

   d) commerce _____

   4 marks

2. Use **two** of the suffixes above and add them to the words below and explain what makes each word tricky to spell.

   a) palace _____

   _____

   b) fierce _____

   _____

   4 marks

Total: [ ] **/21 marks**

Had a go [ ]   **Getting there** [ ]   **Got it!** [ ]

Silent letters

- Recognise and spell words containing silent letters

Letters without a sound

Many words in the English language contain letters that do not make a sound; these are **silent letters**. Once upon a time these letters probably were pronounced, but have become 'silent' over time.

Words containing a silent **w** or silent **k** are quite common.

Example

Silent **w**

- write, e.g. I will **write** to you.
- wrong, e.g. The answer was **wrong**.
- wrap, e.g. I will **wrap** up the present.

Silent **k**

- know, e.g. I **know** the answer.
- knot, e.g. I tied a **knot** in the rope.
- knee, e.g. I hurt my **knee** when I fell.

It can be seen from the examples above that the silent **w** is always followed by the letter **r** (which is the first sound pronounced in the word), and the silent **k** is always followed by the letter **n** (also the first sound pronounced in the word).

Similarly, words with a silent **g** always have an **n** following the silent letter (and this is the first sound pronounced in the word).

Example

Silent **g**

- gnome, e.g. We have a **gnome** in the garden.
- gnaw, e.g. The dogs **gnaw** on their bones.
- gnarled, e.g. The tree had a **gnarled** trunk.

While the examples above all appear at the start of words, silent letters can also appear inside words, or at the end of words.

Example

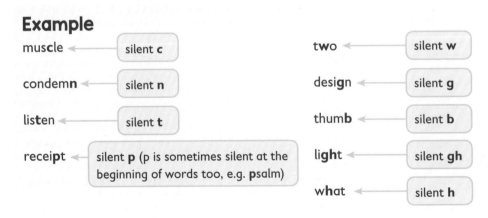

muscle ←	silent **c**
condemn ←	silent **n**
listen ←	silent **t**
receipt ←	silent **p** (p is sometimes silent at the beginning of words too, e.g. **p**salm)

two ←	silent **w**
design ←	silent **g**
thumb ←	silent **b**
light ←	silent **gh**
what ←	silent **h**

Words with silent letters just have to be learned.

> ### Remember
>
> Many silent letters exist from the original spelling and/or pronunciation of the word, often from hundreds of years ago.

> ### Key word
>
> - silent letter

Challenge 1

1. Write the silent letter in each word.

    thumb ☐ **gnat** ☐ **knit** ☐ **wreck** ☐

    4 marks

2. Complete the following:

    a) A silent b at the end of a word is preceded by the letter _____

    b) A silent g is followed by the letter _____

    c) A silent k is followed by the letter _____

    d) A silent w is followed by the letter _____ or _____

    4 marks

Challenge 2

1. Add the correct silent letter that is missing from each word.

    a) lam_____   b) _____ren   c) colum_____

    d) s_____ene   e) _____ hole   f) si_____n

    6 marks

2. What is the meaning of each of the words below? Use a dictionary to help you.

    a) gnat _____

    b) gnash _____

    2 marks

Challenge 3

1. Underline the silent letter in each word then write a sentence containing that word.

    a) calm _____

    _____

    b) hymn _____

    _____

    c) climb _____

    _____

    d) design _____

    _____

    e) ascend _____

    _____

    f) aisle _____

    _____

    6 marks

2. Use the clues to complete the words using the correct letters.

    a) The bones on the back of the hand at the base of the fingers. _____n u _____ k l e s

    b) Something on the roadside giving information. s _____ _____ n

    c) The response to a question. _____ n s _____ e r

    d) He had a new watch on his _____ _____ i s t.

    e) They called a p l u _____ _____ _____ r to repair the leak.

    5 marks

    Total: ☐ /27 marks

Had a go ☐   **Getting there** ☐   **Got it!** ☐

Homophones and near-homophones

- Understand what homophones are and be able to use homophones, near-homophones and other confusing words correctly in sentences

Homophones

Homophones are words that sound the same but have different spellings and meanings.

The words, '*the King had a long reign*' has a different meaning to '*the King had a long rein*'.

'Reign' means how long the king was king for.

But if the full sentence said, '*The king had a long rein in his hand.*' this would probably refer to him holding the rein of a horse.

When reading, it is important to look out for homophones as the correct meaning of a word is important for the overall meaning of the text. When writing, you need to ensure you use the correct word otherwise the meaning of your writing may be changed.

Tip

When reading, read the whole sentence to help understand the context in which a word is being used.

Example

- **aisle** and **isle**

  It was on the cereal **aisle** in the shop.

  I went to a tropical **isle** with palm trees.

- **draft** and **draught**

  I read the first **draft** of her story.

  There is a **draught** from under the door.

- **descent** and **dissent**

  It was a tricky **descent** down the mountain.

  They showed their **dissent** at the idea.

- **guest** and **guessed**

  A famous **guest** came to stay.

  Nobody **guessed** the answer.

Tip

Use a dictionary if you are unsure about which word to use.

Other confusing words

Near-homophones are words that sound *almost* the same but have different spellings and meanings.

Sometimes the root of the word is the same, but the word class is different.

Example

advi**ce** = a noun

They needed **advice** about the best computer to buy.

advi**se** = a verb

The shop assistant came to **advise** them.

Sometimes the word meaning is completely different.

Example

precede (means 'to come before')

The letter a **precedes** b in the alphabet.

proceed (means 'to begin or move forward')

They decided to turn left then **proceed** along the lane.

Remember

It is important not to get homophones mixed up in your writing, otherwise your writing might not make sense.

Key words

- homophone
- near-homophone

1. Look at the underlined words. Write the correct homophone beneath each.

   a) The children all went to choir **practise**.

   b) Sam saw Sue run **passed** the window.

   c) Mobile phones were **band** in school.

   d) She knew her **farther** would be very proud.

4 marks

1. Underline the correct homophone in each sentence.

   a) They ate **cereal / serial** for breakfast.

   b) I counted twenty cows in the **heard / herd**.

   c) Dan read the poem **allowed / aloud** to the class.

   d) She bought the wedding dress from the **bridle / bridal** shop.

4 marks

2. Underline the correct near-homophone in each sentence.

   a) Nobody listened to the **advise / advice** given to them.

   b) She connected to the internet using her **device / devise**.

   c) They were very **wary / weary** of the vicious dog.

   d) He was told to **precede / proceed** to his departure gate.

4 marks

1. Write a sentence using each of the words provided. Use a dictionary to help you.

   a) ascent

   _____

   _____

   b) assent

   _____

   _____

2 marks

2. Complete each explanation below:

   a) A sentence using the word **dissent** would be about _____

   _____

   b) A sentence using the word **descent** would be about _____

   _____

2 marks

Total: [   ] / 16 marks

Had a go [ ]   **Getting there** [ ]   **Got it!** [ ]

53

Using a dictionary

- **Use a dictionary to check the spellings and meanings of words**

Finding words

The words in a **dictionary** are in alphabetical order, which makes them easier to find. The alphabetical order then extends to the second, third and fourth letters and so on.

Example

ice

identity

igloo

ignorant

ignore

ill

illegal

ice is the first of these words because the second letter '**c**' alphabetically comes before the second letter '**d**' in **identity**. For the same reason, identity comes before **igloo**.

igloo comes before **ignorant** because, although the second letter is the same, the third letter l comes before n alphabetically.

The order of **ignorant** and **ignore** is based on the sixth letter, with 'a'.

ill comes before **illegal** because it only has three letters.

Knowing the first letter or first two or three letters of a word can make it easier to find the word in the dictionary. Even just knowing the initial letters can help you to find a word in a dictionary.

Definitions

If you are unsure of the meaning of a word, or of the exact word to use in your writing, the dictionary **definition** will help. The definition is the meaning of the word. Many words in the English language have more than one meaning and often represent more than one class of word.

Abbreviations are also given in a dictionary, such as *adj*, *adv*, *n* or *v* (meaning **adjective**, **adverb**, **noun** or **verb**), to indicate word class.

Example

| drink | *v* | to take liquid into the mouth and swallow |
| | *n* | a liquid that can be swallowed by drinking |

The word **drink** can be a verb or noun and each word class has its own definition.

scale	*n*	1. markings indicating a quantity on a measuring device
		2. the protective covering on the skin of fish and reptiles
		3. a series of musical notes
scale	*v*	to climb up something, e.g. a mountain or building

There are four different definitions given for the word **scale**. Three of them are nouns and one is a verb.

Key words

- dictionary
- definition
- adjective
- adverb
- noun
- verb

Challenge 1

1. Write the numbers 1–6 under the words to show the order in which they would appear in a dictionary.

   a) **silly**   **silliness**   **sincere**   **sinner**   **sincerity**   **since**

   [ ]   [ ]   [ ]   [ ]   [ ]   [ ]

   b) **wish**   **wishful**   **wash**   **wise**   **wisely**   **wisdom**

   [ ]   [ ]   [ ]   [ ]   [ ]   [ ]

   [ ] 2 marks

Challenge 2

1. Use a dictionary to find the different word classes of each word.

   a) skirt   _____ and _____

   b) pocket   _____ and _____ and _____

   c) oil   _____ and _____

   d) fine   _____ and _____ and _____ and _____

   e) drink   _____ and _____

   [ ] 13 marks

Challenge 3

1. Write a dictionary definition for each of the homophones and near-homophones below. Give the word class of each word.

   a) **precede**   _____

   _____

   word class: _____

   b) **proceed**   _____

   _____

   word class: _____

   c) **principal**   _____

   _____

   word class: _____ and _____

   d) **principle**   _____

   _____

   word class: _____

   e) **stationary**   _____

   _____

   word class: _____

   f) **stationery**   _____

   _____

   word class: _____

   [ ] 12 marks

   Total: [ ] **/27 marks**

   Had a go [ ]   **Getting there** [ ]   **Got it!** [ ]

Audience and purpose

- Understand how to plan a piece of writing
- Take account of audience and purpose when writing

Planning

Before writing, it is important to **plan** what your writing will be about, the plot of your story or the information your text will contain. A plan will often be split into sections to help form ideas for different paragraphs, story sections or parts of a non-fiction text.

For each part of the plan, it is a good idea to write key words and phrases too. These can either be descriptive (for example, for characters and settings) or key information (for non-fiction texts). Before or during the writing of the text, some of the ideas in your plan might be moved around or added to.

Who is it for?

It is important to consider **audience** – who the text is for. There is little point in writing a very technical non-fiction piece about trains if the audience is pre-school children. Thinking about the audience will help you consider the content and the type of language you use.

Example

- A letter or email to a friend about plans for the weekend will be more chatty than a letter or email to a local store asking them to sponsor the school sports day.
- A story for your teacher to read will have more advanced language and ideas than a story for a three-year-old.

What is it for?

As well as considering the audience, it is essential to think about the **purpose** of the writing – *what* it is for.

Example

- Is it a **story** to excite and entertain the reader?
  Then it must contain ideas and language that make it exciting and entertaining.
- Is it a **non-fiction text** giving facts and information?
  Then it must contain the key information but must do so in a way that makes the information easy to find in the text.
- Is it an **instructional** text?
  Then it must contain clear steps which make the instructions as easy as possible to follow. It could perhaps include a bullet pointed list of steps.
- Is it a **recount** of events (a chronological report)?
  Then it must contain key events in the order in which they occurred.
- Is it a newspaper **article**?
  Then it must contain the key information that tells the news story.

Challenge 1

1. Draw lines to match each extract to the audience.

a) Racer was a red car. She was fast. The other cars loved Racer. Every day she would speed around the track. Her red paint was bright.

b) Her stomach churned. She wanted to get out of the car, but she could not let nerves win. Her first motor race was about to begin.

c) Dear Sir or Madam, I would like to know if it would be possible for one of your motor racing teams to visit our school. We have been reading…

Teenager

Somebody in charge of motor racing

A small child

3 marks

Challenge 2

1. Draw lines to match each text extract to the purpose of the writing.

a) Mix the ingredients together.
Put the mixture in a cake tin.

b) Swallows are migratory birds.
They fly to warmer climates in winter.

c) First, we visited the old workhouse.
Next, we went to see the sleeping quarters.

d) The police were called to the address and a 34-year-old was arrested for hiding stolen goods.

e) Smokey was quite a sight and surely the strangest looking dragon ever seen. He was odd yet magnificent.

Information text

Fiction story

Newspaper report

Instructions

Recount of events

5 marks

Challenge 3

1. Think about how the content of a story for a four-year-old would be different from the content of a story written for your teacher.

Write at least two different features for each in the table below. Think about the features and language used.

Story for four-year-old	Story for teacher

4 marks

Total: ☐ / 12 marks

Had a go ☐   **Getting there** ☐   **Got it!** ☐

Organising writing

- Understand the importance of paragraphs
- Structure text into clear paragraphs

Paragraphs

Paragraphs are used to help organise writing. Sentences within a paragraph share the same topic or idea.

A paragraph about something a character is doing might be kept separate from a paragraph about how it made another character feel. In this case, the action of one character is separated from the reaction of another.

A paragraph describing a setting might be followed by a separate paragraph about how a character feels in that setting.

If all ideas are written in one paragraph, those ideas can all become muddled together and therefore become less clear to the reader. So it's important to break up your writing into appropriate paragraphs.

Remember

When planning, think about the content you want in each paragraph.

Start a new paragraph when the idea or focus of your writing changes.

Example

For thousands of years, humans had dreamed of flying. They had watched birds and made many unsuccessful attempts to copy them. In 1903, the Wright brothers finally became the first to achieve a controlled aircraft flight. They designed and built their own aircraft and stayed in the air for 59 seconds in that first flight. **Soon they had improved the design and started selling planes in Europe then in the United States. A new era for transport had begun.**

The information in blue makes a good introductory paragraph, giving a little background information and letting the reader know that the text is about humans flying.	The information in green is about the Wright brothers being the first to fly a plane. This is a different idea than the information before and after. It would work better as a separate paragraph.	The information in purple provides further information about the Wright brothers and ends with words that might lead to another paragraph or section of text.

There is a lot of information and ideas in the text above.

Separating it into three paragraphs would help each idea to stand out on its own and would result in a more organised text.

It would also help the reader to find information by recognising the main content of each paragraph.

Tip

Look at paragraphs in texts you read. Try to spot why a new paragraph has been used instead of continuing with the original paragraph.

How to show paragraphs in writing

Paragraphs are shown in writing by:

- indenting the first line of the paragraph and/or
- leaving a line space before starting a new paragraph.

Key word

- paragraph

1. Write each piece of information in the correct column of the table to show whether it belongs in paragraph 1 or paragraph 2.

She was a kind lady.   **She was a great artist.**

She painted trees and plants.   **She enjoyed spending time in the countryside.**

She was quiet and reserved.   **She used oil paints.**

Paragraph 1: The person	Paragraph 2: The painter

6 marks

1. Choose three consecutive paragraphs from a book. Explain briefly how each paragraph differs and what the main idea is in each.

_____

_____

_____

_____

_____

_____

3 marks

1. Compose a short piece of text about yourself, split into two paragraphs.

_____

_____

_____

_____

_____

_____

_____

2 marks

2. Explain why you have chosen to split the text above in the way you have.

_____

_____

_____

1 mark

Total: [ ] / 12 marks

Had a go [ ]   **Getting there** [ ]   **Got it!** [ ]

Settings and characters

- **Effectively describe settings and characters in writing**

Settings

Describing the **setting**, or settings, for a story is important. It helps the reader to understand the story in terms of where the action is happening and allows them to picture it in their mind.

When describing settings, try to use a setting that is familiar to you. This will help it to be more convincing for the reader, as the setting is based on real life experience.

Example

This is a description of a windy playground.

> An icy wind raced across the stark, grey playground, biting at uncovered fingers and ears. Leafless, soulless trees creaked and offered no protection. Children in twos and threes stood together with their backs to the gale. A few brave souls charged at the wind, mouths wide, eyes watering, beneath the darkness of the gathering clouds.

The author of this text has created a vivid description of the setting. The writer obviously knows what it is like in a cold and windy playground and knows that some children will huddle together while others race around. The author has clearly felt the wind biting at fingers and ears. This description makes it easy for readers to picture – or visualise – the setting.

> **Tip**
>
> Think about settings and characters that you already know. Describing some of their features is easier than making up different places or people.

Characters

As with settings, effective descriptions of **characters** are essential in a story. Readers need to be able to visualise characters and understand their behaviour and this comes from good description. Once again, base the characteristics being described on a familiar person, or a combination of different people.

Example

He was a tall man. He was skinny and pale and mean-looking.

> The first description tells us basic 'facts' about the character.

Standing at more than 2 metres tall, the pale, skinny man had dark, mean eyes.

> The second description adds a bit more detail stating how tall he was and that his eyes were dark and mean.

The towering man had to bend his head and back to pass through the doorway. His height looked even greater because he was so thin. Above skinny legs sat a skinny body and a small thin face. A meanness lurked in his small, dark eyes.

> The third description adds interesting vocabulary (towering) and illustrates how tall he was by describing him bending to pass through the doorway. Further detail is added to give a sense of how skinny he was. The mean look is described as 'lurking' which might also relate to the character himself.

It is helpful if the description of a character matches with the role of the character in the story. For example, a kind friendly person, always looking after others would not necessarily make a suitable 'bad' character (although other characteristics could be developed as the story goes on – not everyone is as they seem at first).

> **Key words**
>
> - setting
> - character

Challenge 1

1. a) Think of a place you know. Think of a list of at least three words or phrases to describe that setting and write them down.

_____

_____

   b) Think of a person you know. Think of a list of at least three words or phrases to describe that character's appearance.

_____

_____

   c) Think of the same person. Think of a list of at least three words or phrases to describe that character's personality.

_____

_____

9 marks

Challenge 2

1. Replace the underlined words and phrases with more effective descriptions.

> An eagle <u>flew</u> overhead in large circles.
>
> Eventually, it <u>flew to the ground</u> taking a rabbit from long grass. Mountains cast long shadows over an even darker lake. All around stood <u>hills and mountains</u>.

_____

_____

_____

3 marks

Challenge 3

1. Describe a creepy setting in a paragraph of at least four sentences.

_____

_____

_____

_____

_____

4 marks

2. Describe a kind and gentle character in a paragraph of at least four sentences.

_____

_____

_____

_____

_____

4 marks

Total: ☐ /20 marks

Had a go ☐   **Getting there** ☐   **Got it!** ☐

Editing and proofreading

- Improve writing through editing
- Proofread writing for spelling and punctuation errors

Improving writing

Editing your writing means carefully reading your text and then making improvements to various aspects of it.

Think about the following:

- Does your writing say what you wanted it to say?
- Is the information or story how you wanted it to be?
- Does it follow your plan?
- Have you used interesting or subject-specific vocabulary?
- Does it make sense?
- Are any changes needed to sentence structure, including vocabulary, grammar and punctuation, or to clarify meaning?
- Do your vocabulary choices or descriptions convey the meaning that you intended?
- Is there **cohesion** between sentences and paragraphs? Do the sentences and paragraphs link together well and make sense in the way in which they follow on from each other?

You might decide that you want to change the order of some ideas, sentences and paragraphs if it makes the writing more effective.

It is worth spending some time considering whether you could put across the same message in a different way, and then decide which way sounds most effective.

Proofreading

Proofreading a text means checking for spelling, grammar and punctuation errors. It is also an opportunity to notice any other errors that were not corrected when editing.

Proofreading your own writing is tricky because you already know what the text says. It might help you to read the text out loud, or to ask someone else to proofread it too.

Try to be systematic when proofreading:

- look at each word to check spellings
- then look at each sentence to make sure it is grammatically correct
- then check your punctuation for accuracy.

> ### Remember
>
> Grab the reader's attention by using interesting and exciting vocabulary.

> ### Tip
>
> Use a dictionary to check any spellings you are unsure of.

> ### Tip
>
> When checking spelling, it can sometimes help to read the text backwards (from the end) so that you only read each word and not the whole sentence.

> ### Key words
>
> - editing
> - cohesion
> - proofreading

1. Proofread the text. Circle each spelling and punctuation error.

> The Orient Express is a train wich carrys passengers in great luxury across europe.
>
> For over 100 years, the rich and famus have travelled to romantic citys such as paris
>
> and Venice aboard the train. Would you like to traval in such style. It comes at a
>
> high price, with some tikets costing thousands of pounds

10 marks

1. Edit each of the sentences below to make them more interesting.

a) It was a nice day.

_____

_____

b) They stood under a big tree.

_____

_____

c) I liked the food.

_____

_____

3 marks

1. Edit the passage below by thinking how you could use different words and sentence structure to make it more interesting.

> The train is very posh. It has bedrooms with nice beds and gold taps on the sinks. There is a restaurant with nice views and expensive food. The tickets cost lots of money. A journey on the Orient Express is lovely.

_____

_____

_____

_____

_____

_____

_____

_____

_____

5 marks

Total: [ ] / 18 marks

Had a go [ ]   **Getting there** [ ]   **Got it!** [ ]

Progress test 3

1. Draw lines to match each word with the correct prefix.

   over   **un**   **dis**   **il**

   agreement   **related**   **luminate**   **heat**

4 marks

2. Read the passage below then find and copy an example of each type of figurative language.

   It was a beautiful flight. As the afternoon turned to dusk, the prairie beneath became a red carpet. There was a whoosh of the flame as more heat was added to the balloon, keeping them floating for longer. Sunset was moments away but the glowing golden globe of the balloon was like an even closer, more magnificent sun right above their heads.

   a) **Metaphor** _____

   _____

   b) **Onomatopoeia** _____

   c) **Simile** _____

   _____

   d) **Alliteration** _____

4 marks

3. Use a dictionary to find the different word classes of each word.

   a) **surround**   _____ and _____

   b) **screen**   _____ and _____

   c) **alert**   _____ and _____ and _____

   d) **hand**   _____ and _____

4 marks

4. Circle the correct homophones in the following sentences.

   a) Jay had to go to football **practice** / **practise** after school.

   b) I wasn't sure I had **herd** / **heard** the teacher correctly.

   c) We need to get up early in the **mourning** / **morning** to go on holiday.

   d) The **whether** / **weather** forecast was showing rain for the weekend.

4 marks

5. Write a definition for each homophone. Use a dictionary to help you.

a) **draft**

_____

_____

b) **draught**

_____

_____

c) **peace**

_____

_____

d) **piece**

_____

_____

4 marks

6. Add a prefix to each underlined word so that each sentence makes sense.

a) Daisy lost a mark because she had _____ <u>spelled</u> a word in the spelling test.

b) The magician made the rabbits vanish and then made them _____ <u>appear</u>.

c) James said that he would _____ <u>own</u> his brother if he did not stop being silly.

d) The heat from the fire had caused the plastic bottle to _____ <u>form</u>.

4 marks

7. Add the endings -cious, -tious, -cial or -tial to form a new word, making any necessary spelling adjustments. Write the word class of the original word and the word class of the new word. Use a dictionary if you are unsure.

a) **fiction** _____

Changes from a _____ to a _____

b) **part** _____

Changes from a _____ to a _____

c) **vice** _____

Changes from a _____ to a _____

d) **finance** _____

Changes from a _____ to a _____

8 marks

8. Choose from the options given to state the purpose of each text extract.

story   persuasive text   recount   instructions   report

a)

Next, we went to the beach. After that we had an ice cream.

_____

b)

> Two children, both aged 8, were paddling at Heaton Beach when they saw the man. They witnessed him get into the boat, start the engine and drive away.

_____

c)

> At last they felt coolness of water on their feet. They no longer minded the hot sun on their backs as they could now dive into deeper, refreshing water. It felt glorious.

_____

d)

> First, take the sun cream from your bag then squeeze a little onto your hands. Next, rub the sun cream all over your body and face. After that, lie on your towel and enjoy sunbathing.

_____

e)

> It is important to wear sun cream to protect your skin. Do you really want to get sunburned? It is sore, uncomfortable and very bad for you.

_____

5 marks

9. **Edit each of the sentences below to make them more interesting.**

a) The attic was spooky.

_____

_____

b) The rain was heavy.

_____

_____

c) The ride was fun.

_____

_____

3 marks

10. **Add a different prefix to each word below then write a sentence containing the new word.**

a) _____ **understanding**

_____

_____

b) _____ **satisfied**

_____

_____

c) _____ **kind**

_____

_____

d) _____ school

_____

_____

4 marks

11. Label each statement below as fact (F) or opinion (O).

a) Strawberries are delicious. ☐

b) Spain is a country in Europe. ☐

c) Tom is 154cm tall. ☐

d) Flowers smell beautiful. ☐

e) Tim's dog is cute. ☐

f) The bus is exactly 5 minutes late. ☐

6 marks

12. Choose one fact and one opinion from your answers to question 11 and explain the reasons for your answers.

_____

_____

_____

2 marks

13. Read the text then answer the questions.

Hetty was arguing with her mum. She was always arguing and was quite a spoiled child. Once again, Hetty had not done her homework.

"You must do it Hetty, darling," insisted her mother. "It will help you at school."

"I can't be bothered," snarled Hetty. "If you think it's so important, you do it."

"Oh Hetty, please don't be so rude, darling. Mummy just wants to help you and if you don't do it you might no longer be the cleverest in your class," said mum rather helplessly.

"I don't care!" yelled the daughter, storming from the room and slamming the door.

a) What word is used to summarise Hetty?

_____

b) What does Mum say will happen if Hetty does not do her homework?

_____

c) Summarise the text in no more than two sentences.

_____

_____

_____

3 marks

Total: ☐ /55 marks

Comparing and ordering fractions

- Recognise mixed numbers and improper fractions and convert from one to the other
- Identify and name equivalent fractions of a given fraction
- Compare and order fractions

Mixed numbers and improper fractions

A **mixed number** uses whole numbers and **fractions**, e.g. $6\frac{2}{3}$ and $10\frac{7}{10}$

An **improper fraction** records numbers greater than or equal to one as a fraction only, e.g. $\frac{20}{3}$ and $\frac{107}{10}$

Example

Change $2\frac{3}{4}$ (a mixed number) to an improper fraction.

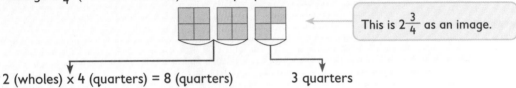

> This is $2\frac{3}{4}$ as an image.

2 (wholes) × 4 (quarters) = 8 (quarters)   3 quarters

So, 8 (quarters) + 3 (more quarters) = 11 (quarters)

$2\frac{3}{4}$ = 11 quarters: $\frac{11}{4}$

Change $\frac{14}{5}$ (an improper fraction) to a mixed number.

$\frac{14}{5} = \frac{1}{5} + \frac{1}{5} + \frac{1}{5} + \frac{1}{5} + \frac{1}{5} + \frac{1}{5} + \frac{1}{5} + \frac{1}{5} + \frac{1}{5} + \frac{1}{5} + \frac{1}{5} + \frac{1}{5} + \frac{1}{5} + \frac{1}{5}$

Making groups of five-fifths would give the number of whole numbers because $\frac{5}{5} = 1$

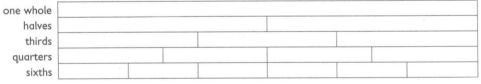

> There are two groups of five-fifths with four-fifths left over.

So, $14 ÷ 5 = 2\ r\ 4 = 2\frac{4}{5}$

Equivalent fractions

A whole can be divided into fractions in different ways. This is a fraction wall:

| one whole |
| halves |
| thirds |
| quarters |
| sixths |

> $\frac{1}{2}$ is the same as $\frac{2}{4}$, is the same as $\frac{3}{6}$

Check and extend the pattern of the **numerators** and **denominators**:

$\frac{1}{2} = \frac{2}{4} = \frac{3}{6} = \frac{4}{8} = \frac{5}{10} = \frac{6}{12} = \ldots$

These are **equivalent fractions**. They can be found using multiplication and division.

Example

$\overset{\times\,3}{\frac{1}{2} = \frac{3}{6}}$ Multiply by the same number. $\overset{\div\,5}{\frac{15}{20} = \frac{3}{4}}$ Divide by a common factor.

To compare or order fractions, find equivalent fractions first.

Example

$\frac{3}{4} > \frac{7}{12}$ because $\frac{3}{4} = \frac{9}{12}$ so $\frac{9}{12} > \frac{7}{12}$

Key words

- mixed number
- fraction
- improper fraction
- numerator
- denominator
- equivalent fraction

Challenge 1

1. Change these mixed numbers to improper fractions.

   a) $2\frac{1}{2} = \dfrac{\boxed{}}{2}$

   b) $3\frac{1}{3} = \dfrac{\boxed{}}{3}$

   2 marks

2. Change these improper fractions to mixed numbers.

   a) $\dfrac{7}{2} = $ _____

   b) $\dfrac{11}{3} = $ _____

   2 marks

3. Find the missing denominator in these equivalent fractions.

   a) $\dfrac{3}{5} = \dfrac{9}{\boxed{}}$

   b) $\dfrac{3}{8} = \dfrac{12}{\boxed{}}$

   2 marks

4. Circle the larger fraction in each pair.

   a) $\dfrac{2}{3}$ $\dfrac{11}{15}$

   b) $\dfrac{4}{5}$ $\dfrac{13}{20}$

   c) $\dfrac{1}{4}$ $\dfrac{5}{12}$

   3 marks

Challenge 2

1. Change these mixed numbers to improper fractions.

   a) $6\frac{3}{5} = $ _____

   b) $4\frac{3}{8} = $ _____

   2 marks

2. Change these improper fractions to mixed numbers.

   a) $\dfrac{23}{4} = $ _____

   b) $\dfrac{27}{8} = $ _____

   2 marks

PS 3. Ben, Tom and Dev share some money. Ben takes $\frac{1}{3}$ of the money, Tom takes $\frac{5}{12}$ and Dev takes $\frac{6}{24}$

Who takes the most money? _____

1 mark

Challenge 3

1. Change the mixed numbers to improper fractions and the improper fractions to mixed numbers.

   a) $7\frac{1}{5} = $ _____

   b) _____ $= \dfrac{29}{6}$

   c) $8\frac{1}{12} = $ _____

   d) _____ $= \dfrac{35}{8}$

   4 marks

2. Circle the smallest fraction.

   a) $\dfrac{4}{5}$ $\dfrac{11}{15}$ $\dfrac{7}{10}$ $\dfrac{13}{20}$

   b) $\dfrac{5}{6}$ $\dfrac{7}{9}$ $\dfrac{11}{12}$ $\dfrac{13}{18}$

   2 marks

PS 3. For a school party, Tara, Nia and Beth each buy 2 pizzas. Tara cuts each of her pizzas into 8 pieces and there are 9 pieces left; Nia cuts hers into 4 pieces each and there are 5 pieces left; Beth cuts hers into 12 pieces each and there are 11 pieces left.

Write the names of the girls in order, showing who has the most pizza left.

_____   _____   _____

1 mark

Total: ☐ /21 marks

Had a go ☐   **Getting there** ☐   **Got it!** ☐

Adding, subtracting and multiplying fractions

- Add and subtract fractions
- Multiply proper fractions and mixed numbers by whole numbers

Adding and subtracting fractions

When adding or subtracting **fractions**, the **denominator** tells you the number of pieces in the whole.

Example

- $\frac{1}{8} + \frac{3}{8} = \frac{4}{8}$

  This is one-eighth add three-eighths. This gives four eighths. Four-eighths is the same as one-half. Giving the answer as $\frac{1}{2}$ means you have reduced the fraction to its **lowest terms**.

To add or subtract fractions, the denominators must be the same.

Example

- $\frac{5}{8} - \frac{1}{4} =$

  This is five-eighths subtract one-quarter. The fractions are different. The denominators need to be the same before the **numerators** can be subtracted, so at least one must be changed by finding the **lowest common multiple**.

  One-quarter can be changed to two eighths. Now two-eighths can be subtracted from five-eighths leaving three-eighths: $\frac{5}{8} - \frac{2}{8} = \frac{3}{8}$

- $\frac{5}{6} - \frac{1}{4} =$

  This is five-sixths subtract one-quarter. Again, the fractions are different and need to be changed by finding the lowest common multiple for each denominator. The lowest common multiple of 4 and 6 is 12

  $\frac{5}{6} = \frac{10}{12}$ and $\frac{1}{4} = \frac{3}{12}$, so $\frac{10}{12} - \frac{3}{12} = \frac{7}{12}$

Multiplying fractions

To multiply **proper fractions** you could use repeated addition, or drawings, or multiply both numerators and then both denominators.

Example

- $\frac{1}{3} \times 5 =$

  Use repeated addition: $\frac{1}{3} + \frac{1}{3} + \frac{1}{3} + \frac{1}{3} + \frac{1}{3} =$

  $\frac{5}{3}$ is an **improper fraction** and can be changed into a **mixed number**: $\frac{5}{3} = 1\frac{2}{3}$

- $\frac{3}{4} \times 6 =$ Use drawings:

  Here are six blocks and each has three-quarters shaded:

  > Altogether, there are 18 quarters shaded.
  > $\frac{3}{4} \times 6 = \frac{18}{4} = 4\frac{2}{4} = 4\frac{1}{2}$

- $\frac{3}{4} \times 6 =$ Use multiplication of the numerator and denominator:

  6 can be written as $\frac{6}{1}$, so $\frac{3}{4} \times \frac{6}{1} = \frac{18}{4} = 4\frac{2}{4} = 4\frac{1}{2}$

Remember

The denominator gives the number of pieces in a whole. It is the numerator that tells how many pieces are to be added or subtracted.

> Here, there are five-thirds: $\frac{5}{3}$

Tip

Use drawings or jottings to help you see the calculation.

Key words

- fraction
- denominator
- lowest terms
- numerator
- lowest common multiple
- proper fraction
- improper fraction
- mixed number

Challenge 1

1. a) $\frac{3}{8} + \frac{2}{8} =$ _____   b) $\frac{5}{12} + \frac{6}{12} =$ _____   c) $\frac{13}{20} - \frac{4}{20} =$ _____

PS 2. Harry cuts a pizza into twelfths. He eats $\frac{3}{12}$ and his friend eats $\frac{4}{12}$

    What fraction of the pizza is left? _____

3. These blocks each have $\frac{2}{3}$ shaded.

    a) Calculate as an improper fraction and a mixed number, $\frac{2}{3} \times 4 =$ _____ = _____

    b) In the same way calculate:

    $\frac{2}{3} \times 2 =$ _____ = _____ $\frac{2}{3} \times 5 =$ _____ = _____ $\frac{2}{3} \times 3 =$ _____ = _____

Challenge 2

1. a) $\frac{3}{5} + \frac{3}{10} =$ _____   b) $\frac{5}{12} + \frac{1}{3} =$ _____   c) $\frac{8}{9} - \frac{2}{3} =$ _____

PS 2. Len makes cakes for a stall at a fete. They are flavoured with vanilla, lemon or strawberry.

    $\frac{3}{8}$ of Len's cakes are vanilla flavoured and $\frac{1}{4}$ are lemon flavoured.

    What fraction are strawberry flavoured? _____

3. This block has $\frac{3}{5}$ shaded.

    Use the drawing to calculate:

    a) $\frac{3}{5} \times 3 =$ _____ = _____   b) $\frac{3}{5} \times 5 =$ _____ = _____   c) $\frac{3}{5} \times 7 =$ _____ = _____

Challenge 3

1. a) $\frac{3}{4} + \frac{1}{3} =$ _____ = _____   b) $\frac{5}{6} + \frac{3}{4} =$ _____ = _____   c) $\frac{2}{3} - \frac{2}{5} =$ _____

PS 2. Find the missing numerators.

    a) $\frac{11}{12} + \frac{\boxed{}}{4} = 1\frac{8}{12}$

    b) $\frac{2}{3} + \frac{\boxed{}}{8} = 1\frac{7}{24}$

    c) $\frac{3}{5} + \frac{\boxed{}}{20} = 1\frac{1}{4}$

3. a) $\frac{3}{8} \times 3 =$ _____ = _____

    b) $\frac{5}{6} \times 5 =$ _____ = _____

Total: [ ] /23 marks

Had a go [ ]   **Getting there** [ ]   **Got it!** [ ]

Fraction and decimal equivalents I

- Read and write decimal numbers as fractions
- Recognise and use tenths, hundredths and thousandths and their decimal equivalents

Fractions

A **fraction** is a number that describes part of a whole and that whole can be of any size, quantity or amount.

The **denominator** – the bottom number of a fraction – gives the number of parts that the whole is divided into. This can be any number, unlike **decimals** which can only record fractions as tenths, hundredths, thousandths and so on.

Fractions as decimal numbers

A fraction can be written as a decimal, but the fraction must be based on a group of ten, so only tenths, hundredths, thousandths and so on can be written as a decimal.

Example

$\frac{3}{10} = 0.3$ $\qquad \frac{9}{100} = 0.09$ $\qquad \frac{7}{1,000} = 0.007$ $\qquad \frac{81}{100} = 0.81$ $\qquad \frac{507}{1,000} = 0.507$

When a fraction is not based on a group of ten, an equivalent fraction is needed that is based on a group of ten.

Example

$\frac{4}{5}$ This fraction is not in the form of tenths or hundredths, so an equivalent fraction is needed:

$$\frac{4}{5} = \frac{8}{10} = 0.8$$

$\frac{23}{25}$ This fraction can be changed to hundredths. The denominator 25 can be multiplied by 4 to make 100 so the numerator must also be multiplied by 4.

$\times 4$

$$\frac{23}{25} = \frac{92}{100} = 0.92$$

$\times 4$

$$\frac{23}{25} = 0.92$$

All fractions must be changed into tenths, hundredths or thousandths to be written as a decimal by finding suitable **equivalent fractions**.

Example

$\frac{2}{5} = \frac{4}{10} = 0.4$

$\frac{3}{4} = \frac{75}{100} = 0.75$

$\frac{9}{25} = \frac{36}{100} = 0.36$

$\frac{7}{8} = \frac{875}{1,000} = 0.875$

> ### Remember
>
> A **decimal point** is used to separate whole numbers from parts of whole numbers, e.g. tenths and hundredths.

Thousands	Hundreds	Tens	Ones	.	Tenths	Hundredths	Thousandths
			0	.	8		
			0	.	9	2	

> ### Key words
>
> - fraction
> - denominator
> - decimal
> - decimal point
> - equivalent fraction

Challenge 1

1. Change these fractions to decimals.

   a) $\frac{7}{10}$ = _____

   b) $\frac{2}{10}$ = _____

   c) $\frac{37}{100}$ = _____

   d) $\frac{93}{100}$ = _____

   e) $\frac{9}{100}$ = _____

   5 marks

2. Change these fractions to decimals.

   a) $\frac{1}{2}$ = _____

   b) $\frac{1}{4}$ = _____

   c) $\frac{1}{5}$ = _____

   3 marks

PS 3. Chen puts $\frac{3}{4}$ of a kilogram of flour on a set of digital scales.

   What is the decimal reading on the scales?

   _____

   1 mark

Challenge 2

1. Change these fractions to decimals.

   a) $\frac{8}{100}$ = _____

   b) $\frac{9}{10}$ = _____

   c) $\frac{29}{100}$ = _____

   d) $\frac{9}{100}$ = _____

   e) $\frac{439}{1,000}$ = _____

   5 marks

2. Change these fractions to decimals.

   a) $\frac{4}{5}$ = _____

   b) $\frac{1}{20}$ = _____

   c) $\frac{33}{50}$ = _____

   3 marks

PS 3. Myra scores $\frac{83}{100}$ in a test. Her score must be written as a decimal so it can be entered into a computer.

   What is Myra's score as a decimal?

   _____

   1 mark

Challenge 3

1. Change these fractions to decimals.

   a) $\frac{73}{100}$ = _____

   b) $\frac{28}{1,000}$ = _____

   c) $\frac{807}{1,000}$ = _____

   d) $\frac{913}{100}$ = _____

   e) $\frac{790}{1,000}$ = _____

   f) $\frac{3441}{1,000}$ = _____

   6 marks

2. Change these fractions to decimals.

   a) $\frac{11}{20}$ = _____

   b) $\frac{49}{50}$ = _____

   c) $\frac{2}{25}$ = _____

   3 marks

PS 3. Max says, "$1\frac{1}{1,000}$ is the same as 1.1"

   Explain why Max is incorrect.

   _____

   _____

   _____

   1 mark

Total: ☐ /28 marks

Had a go ☐   **Getting there** ☐   **Got it!** ☐

Fraction and decimal equivalents 2

- Read and write decimal numbers as fractions
- Recognise and use tenths, hundredths and thousandths and their decimal equivalents

Decimal numbers

10 is ten times larger than 1; 100 is ten times larger than 10 and so on. Similarly, 1 is ten times smaller than 10; 10 is ten times smaller than 100 and so on. This is continued by making 1 ten times smaller. These are **decimal** numbers.

$1 \div 10 = \frac{1}{10}$ ←   This is 0.1 as a decimal number.

$\frac{1}{10} \div 10 = \frac{1}{100}$ ←   This is 0.01 as a decimal number.

$\frac{1}{100} \div 10 = \frac{1}{1,000}$ ←   This is 0.001 as a decimal number.

Decimal numbers as fractions

A decimal number can be changed into a fraction by using the **place value** column titles.

Example

Thousands	Hundreds	Tens	Ones	.	Tenths	Hundredths	Thousandths	
			0	.	3			There is a digit 3 in the tenths column = $\frac{3}{10}$
			0	.	0	9		There are hundredths here. There is a digit 9 in the hundredths column = $\frac{9}{100}$
			0	.	6	1		There are hundredths here. Read off the number of hundredths from the decimal point = $\frac{61}{100}$
			2	.	0	8	7	The 2 wholes will remain as wholes. There are thousandths here. Read off the number of thousandths from the decimal point. = $2\frac{87}{1,000}$ So, the decimal number 2.087 is a mixed fraction.

Sometimes the fractions need to be reduced to their **lowest terms**.

Example

$3\frac{6}{10} = 3\frac{3}{5}$ ←   Use 2 as the **common factor**.

$9\frac{5}{100} = 9\frac{1}{20}$ ←   Use 5 as the common factor.

$17\frac{25}{1,000} = 17\frac{1}{40}$ ←   Use 25 as the common factor.

Remember

When writing a decimal as a **fraction** it must be in the form of tenths, hundredths, thousandths, etc.

Remember

Always use the place value column titles when working with decimal numbers.

Key words

- decimal
- fraction
- place value
- lowest terms
- common factor

Challenge 1

1. Change these decimals to fractions.

   a) 0.3 = _____   b) 0.07 = _____   c) 0.009 = _____

   d) 0.39 = _____   e) 0.19 = _____   f) 0.437 = _____

   6 marks

2. Change these decimals to fractions and write them in their lowest terms.

   a) 0.5 = _____

   b) 0.25 = _____

   c) 0.75 = _____

   3 marks

PS 3. An oil tank has a digital display showing how full it is. The display shows 0.2

   How full is the tank as a fraction? _____

   1 mark

Challenge 2

1. Change these decimals to fractions.

   a) 0.91 = _____   b) 0.817 = _____   c) 0.607 = _____

   d) 10.01 = _____   e) 0.097 = _____   f) 0.777 = _____

   6 marks

2. Change these decimals to fractions and write them in their lowest terms.

   a) 0.025 = _____

   b) 0.05 = _____

   c) 0.92 = _____

   3 marks

PS 3. A film is reviewed by a magazine and given a rating of 4.7 stars.

   What is this rating written as a mixed number?

   _____

   1 mark

Challenge 3

1. Change these decimals to fractions and write them in their lowest terms.

   a) 0.15 = _____   b) 0.48 = _____   c) 0.85 = _____

   d) 0.52 = _____   e) 0.075 = _____   f) 0.125 = _____

   6 marks

2. Change these decimals to mixed numbers and write them in their lowest terms.

   a) 6.6 = _____

   b) 10.95 = _____

   c) 8.16 = _____

   d) 3.125 = _____

   e) 9.72 = _____

   f) 2.375 = _____

   6 marks

PS 3. Jonty has a secret number. He gives some clues about his number: it is a proper fraction and can be written as twenty-fifths; it is greater than 0.5, but less than 0.55; it has two decimal places.

   What is Jonty's secret number? _____

   1 mark

Total: ☐ /33 marks

Had a go ☐   **Getting there** ☐   **Got it!** ☐

75

Decimals

- Round decimals to the nearest whole number and to one decimal place
- Read, write, order and compare numbers with up to three decimal places

Decimal numbers

Decimal numbers have **decimal places**. The first decimal place is the first number after the **decimal point** (dp).

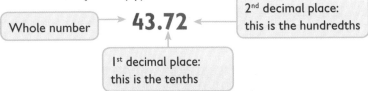

Whole number → **43.72** ← 2nd decimal place: this is the hundredths

1st decimal place: this is the tenths

Remember

Any number without a decimal point is a whole number, but it could still have a decimal point after the ones column, e.g. 43 is also 43.0

Rounding decimal numbers

Decimal numbers can be written to the nearest whole number or to one decimal place.

Example

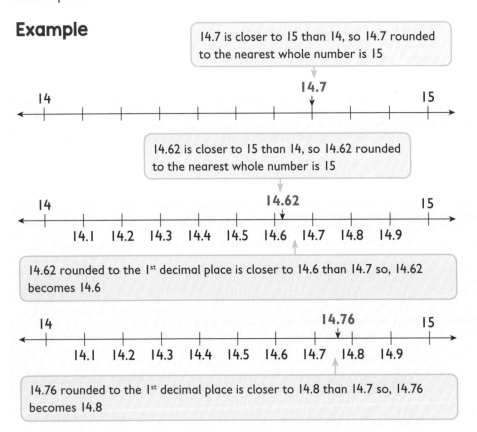

14.7 is closer to 15 than 14, so 14.7 rounded to the nearest whole number is 15

14.62 is closer to 15 than 14, so 14.62 rounded to the nearest whole number is 15

14.62 rounded to the 1st decimal place is closer to 14.6 than 14.7 so, 14.62 becomes 14.6

14.76 rounded to the 1st decimal place is closer to 14.8 than 14.7 so, 14.76 becomes 14.8

Remember

The digit following the rounding instruction is the key to rounding up or down. When rounding to the 1st dp, look at the digit in the 2nd dp; when rounding to the nearest whole number, look at the 1st dp.

Tip

Always check carefully whether a number has a decimal point or not; they can be easy to miss.

Ordering and comparing decimal numbers

Decimal numbers can be compared and ordered using the **place value** of the digits.

Example

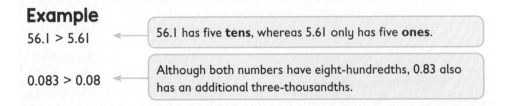

56.1 > 5.61 ← 56.1 has five **tens**, whereas 5.61 only has five **ones**.

0.083 > 0.08 ← Although both numbers have eight-hundredths, 0.83 also has an additional three-thousandths.

Key words

- decimal
- decimal place
- decimal point
- place value

Challenge 1

1. Round these decimals to the nearest whole number.

   a) 6.3 _____

   b) 10.7 _____

   2 marks

2. Write < or > in each box to make these number sentences correct.

   a) 5.6 ☐ 5.27

   b) 14.8 ☐ 1.48

   2 marks

PS 3. Marti is 73.2 cm tall; Nisha is 73.3 cm tall; Tara is 72.9 cm tall and Maria is 73.5 cm tall.

   Who is the tallest?

   _____

   1 mark

Challenge 2

1. Round these decimals to the nearest whole number.

   a) 11.91 _____

   b) 19.7 _____

   2 marks

2. Round these decimals to the 1st decimal place.

   a) 7.07 _____

   b) 25.61 _____

   2 marks

3. Write these decimals in order, smallest first.

   a) 5.61   5.16   6.51   6.15

   _____   _____   _____   _____

   b) 68.87   68.807   68.078   68.708

   _____   _____   _____   _____

   2 marks

PS 4. Josh has £12.76, Mo has £12.74, Samir has £12.68 and Noah has £12.70

   Who has the most?

   _____

   1 mark

Challenge 3

1. Round these decimals to the nearest whole number.

   a) 39.5 _____

   b) 25.255 _____

   2 marks

2. Round these decimals to the 1st decimal place.

   a) 11.96 _____

   b) 52.17 _____

   2 marks

3. Write these decimals in order, smallest first.

   a) 6.452   6.542   6.245   6.254

   _____   _____   _____   _____

   b) 11.1   11.18   11.081   11.018

   _____   _____   _____   _____

   2 marks

PS 4. In a running race, Tia is timed at 14.149 seconds, Jo at 14.492, Lisa at 14.942 and Ola at 14.194

   Who won the race?

   _____

   1 mark

Total: ☐ / 19 marks

Had a go ☐   **Getting there** ☐   **Got it!** ☐

Percentages

- Understand percentages as 'parts per hundred'
- Find fraction and decimal equivalents for percentages
- Solve problems using percentages

Percentages

A **percentage** is a special kind of **fraction**. All percentages as fractions have a **denominator** of 100 but some can then be reduced to their **lowest terms**. Percentages are written with the symbol **%**.

Example

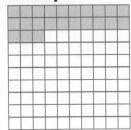

> 23 squares out of 100 squares are shaded. This shows 23%.

> **Remember**
>
> It is easier to write the equivalent decimal of a percentage when using a fraction with a denominator of 100.

Percentages are useful for comparing different amounts by showing them all in the same proportion.

Percentage equivalents

Because a percentage is a kind of fraction with a denominator of 100, it can be written as a **proper fraction** or as an **improper fraction**. This means a percentage can be written as a decimal.

Example

$23\% = \frac{23}{100} = 0.23$ ← As a proper fraction and a decimal

$137\% = \frac{137}{100} = 1.37$ ← As an improper fraction and a decimal

Some percentages, when changed to a fraction, can be reduced to their lowest terms.

Example

$75\% = \frac{75}{100} = \frac{3}{4} = 0.75$

$4\% = \frac{4}{100} = \frac{1}{25} = 0.04$

Solving problems with percentages

If you know simple fraction equivalents of some percentages, it can make solving problems quicker and easier. Try to learn these simple fraction equivalents:

$50\% = \frac{1}{2}$ $25\% = \frac{1}{4}$

$20\% = \frac{1}{5}$ $10\% = \frac{1}{10}$

$75\% = \frac{3}{4}$

> **Key words**
>
> - percentage
> - fraction
> - denominator
> - lowest terms
> - proper fraction
> - improper fraction

Challenge 1

1. Tick the shape that has 25% shaded.

☐ ☐ ☐ ☐

1 mark

2. Write these percentages as fractions.

   a) 29% = _____   b) 87% = _____   c) 43% = _____

   3 marks

3. Write these percentages as decimals.

   a) 67% = _____   b) 9% = _____   c) 99% = _____

   3 marks

PS 4. A school has 120 pupils. 25% of the pupils bring a packed lunch for dinner.

How many pupils bring a packed lunch?

1 mark

Challenge 2

PS 1. Holly must shade 80% of a shape. The shape is divided into 20 equal sections.

How many sections must Holly shade?

1 mark

2. Write each percentage as a fraction in its lowest terms.

   a) 60% = _____   b) 70% = _____   c) 75% = _____   d) 5% = _____

   4 marks

3. Change these decimals to percentages.

   a) 0.57 = _____   b) 0.07 = _____   c) 0.3 = _____

   3 marks

PS 4. Sally earns £240 a week. She gets a pay rise of 5%.

How much extra a week will she earn after her pay rise?

_____

1 mark

Challenge 3

1. Write fraction and decimal equivalents of these percentages.

   a) 15% = _____ = _____   b) 90% = _____ = _____

   4 marks

PS 2. Cory has 1 hour to do his homework. He spends 70% of the time doing maths.

How many minutes does he spend doing his maths homework?

1 mark

PS 3. Jenny has £24 and spends 75% of the money on a book.

What is the cost of the book?

_____

1 mark

PS 4. Dev saved £180, which is $\frac{3}{5}$ of the money he needs for a new computer. Then he finds the cost of the computer is reduced by 50% in a sale. Dev buys the computer at the sale price.

How much will Dev have left over? _____

1 mark

Total: ☐ /24 marks

Had a go ☐   **Getting there** ☐   **Got it!** ☐

79

Converting units of measure

- Solve problems converting units of time
- Convert different units of metric measure for length, mass and capacity

Units of time

The basic units of time are:

60 seconds	=	1 minute
60 minutes	=	1 hour
24 hours	=	1 day
7 days	=	1 week
12 months	=	1 year
365 days	=	1 year

Remember

Having an instant recall of all these facts makes calculations a lot easier.

The number of days in each month varies.

January	31	April	30	July	31	October	31
February	28	May	31	August	31	November	30
March	31	June	30	September	30	December	31

In a leap year, which occurs every 4 years, there is an extra day in February. This is 29th February.

Converting units

To convert the smaller unit to the larger unit, divide by the number of smaller units. To convert the larger unit to the smaller unit, multiply by the number of smaller units.

Example

- Convert 240 minutes into hours:

  240 (minutes) ÷ 60 (number of units per larger unit) = **4** (hours)

- Convert 3 days into hours:

  3 (days) × 24 (number of units per larger unit) = **72** (hours)

Units of metric measure

The basic **metric measures** are:

Length:	10 millimetres	=	1 centimetre	10 mm	=	1 cm
	100 centimetres	=	1 metre	100 cm	=	1 m
	1,000 metres	=	1 kilometre	1,000 m	=	1 km
Mass:	1,000 grams	=	1 kilogram	1,000 g	=	1 kg
	1,000 kilograms	=	1 tonne	1,000 kg	=	1 t
Capacity:	1 millilitre	=	1 cubic centimetre	1 ml	=	$1 cm^3$
	1,000 millilitres	=	1 litre	1,000 ml	=	1 l
	100 centilitres	=	1 litre	100 cl	=	1 l

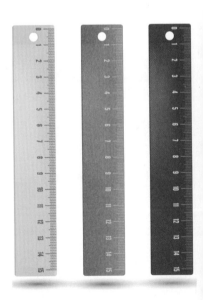

To convert the smaller unit to the larger unit, divide by the number of smaller units. To convert the larger unit to the smaller unit, multiply by the number of smaller units.

Example

- Convert 560 cm into metres:
  560 (cm) ÷ 100 (number of units per larger unit) = **5.6** (m)
- Convert 6.05 kg into grams:
  6.05 (kg) × 1,000 (number of units per larger unit) = **6,050** (g)

Key word

- metric measures

Challenge 1

1. Change the metric measures.

   a) 500 cm = _____ m
   b) 5,000 ml = _____ litres
   c) 6 kg = _____ g
   d) 7 km = _____ m
   e) $\frac{1}{2}$ m = _____ cm

   5 marks

2. Change these units of time.

   a) 360 seconds = _____ minutes
   b) 28 days = _____ weeks
   c) 4 hours = _____ minutes

   3 marks

PS 3. Sally's birthday is on Tuesday, 29th April. She is having a birthday party on the next Saturday.

   What is the date of Sally's birthday party?

   _____

   1 mark

PS 4. Keira spends $2\frac{1}{2}$ hours doing her homework. She divides her time equally between 3 tasks.

   How long does Keira spend on each task?

   _____

   1 mark

Challenge 2

1. Change the metric measures.

   a) 630 cm = _____ m
   b) 8,300 ml = _____ litres
   c) 9.6 kg = _____ g
   d) 7.25 km = _____ m
   e) $\frac{1}{4}$ litre = _____ ml

   5 marks

2. Change these units of time.

   a) $5\frac{1}{2}$ minutes = _____ seconds
   b) 7 days = _____ hours
   c) $7\frac{1}{2}$ hours = _____ minutes

   3 marks

PS 3. Javid drives for 45 minutes, takes a break for 15 minutes and then drives for twice as long.

   How long is his journey in hours and minutes? _____ hrs _____ mins

   1 mark

PS 4. It is 29th March. Nia goes on holiday in 72 hours for 7 days.

   What is the date Nia will return?

   _____

   1 mark

Challenge 3

1. Change the metric measures.

   a) 9750 cm = _____ m
   b) 10.2 litres = _____ ml
   c) 12.75 km = _____ m
   d) $\frac{3}{4}$ kg = _____ g
   e) 5050 g = _____ kg

   5 marks

PS 2. Lexie spends $2\frac{1}{2}$ hours watching a film, 45 minutes tidying up and $\frac{1}{4}$ hour on the phone.

   How long does she spend on all three tasks?

   _____

   1 mark

PS 3. The 1st May is a Thursday. What day is the 1st June? _____

   1 mark

   Total: [ ] **/27 marks**

Had a go [ ] **Getting there** [ ] **Got it!** [ ]

81

Equivalent metric and imperial measures

- **Understand and use metric and imperial units of measure**

Imperial measures

Imperial measures are an older system of measures that were used before **metric measures**. Some are still used so it is important to be able to convert between imperial and metric units.

Converting involves multiplying or dividing by the number of equivalent units, e.g. 1 inch is about 2.5 cm, so:

- multiply inches by 2.5 to find an equivalent number of centimetres
- divide centimetres by 2.5 to find an equivalent number of inches.

> **Remember**
>
> It is helpful to know the approximate equivalents between the imperial and metric units.

Length

Imperial measures of length:

- 12 inches (ins) = 1 foot (ft)
- 3 feet (ft) = 1 yard (yd)
- 1 inch is about 2.5 cm
- 1 yard is about 90 cm

Example

Convert 8 feet into cm

8 feet × 12 (number of inches in 1 foot) = 96 ins

96 ins × 2.5 (number of units per imperial unit) is about **240 cm**

Mass

Imperial measures of mass:

- 16 ounces (oz) = 1 pound (lb)
- 14 pounds (lbs) = 1 stone (st)
- 1 pound is about 450 grams or 0.45 kg

Example

Convert 4 pounds into kg

4 lbs × 0.45 (number of units per imperial unit) is about **1.8 kg**

Convert 8 kg into pounds

8 × 2.2 is about **17.6 lbs**

> To convert kilograms into pounds, multiply by 2.2

Capacity

Imperial measures of capacity:

- 8 pints (pts) = 1 gallon (gal)
- 1 pint is about 560 millilitres.
- 1 gallon is about 4.5 litres.

Example

Convert 40 litres into gallons:

40 litres ÷ 4.5 (number of units per imperial unit) is about **8.9 gallons**

> **Key words**
>
> - imperial measures
> - metric measures

1. Find the approximate measures.

   a)   5 inches is about _____ centimetres

   b)   6 gallons is about _____ litres

   c)   3 pounds is about _____ grams

   3 marks

PS 2.   Laura measures a line as 18 inches long.

   Approximately how long is this in centimetres? _____

   1 mark

PS 3.   Max finds an old recipe book. One of the recipes says to use 16 ounces of flour.

   Approximately what is this mass in grams? _____

   1 mark

PS 4.   Kobi finds an old water container. It holds 3 gallons.

   Approximately what is this capacity in litres? _____

   1 mark

1. Find the approximate measures.

   a)   12 yards is about _____ metres

   b)   9 gallons is about _____ litres

   c)   4 pounds is about _____ grams

   3 marks

PS 2.   Ben says his garden is 40 yards long.

   Approximately how long is this in metres? _____

   1 mark

PS 3.   Katie's new baby has a mass of $2\frac{1}{2}$ kilograms.

   Approximately what is this mass in pounds? _____

   1 mark

PS 4.   Layla reads that old school desks were $3\frac{1}{2}$ feet wide.

   Approximately how long is this in centimetres? _____

   1 mark

1. Find the approximate measures.

   a)   5 inches is about _____ centimetres

   b)   6 gallons is about _____ litres

   c)   8 pounds is about _____ kilograms

   3 marks

PS 2.   Tara says, "I am 5 feet tall and have a mass of 4 stones".

   a)   Approximately how tall is Tara in centimetres? _____

   b)   Approximately what is her mass in kilograms? _____

   2 marks

PS 3.   Mo's car's petrol tank can hold 15 gallons.

   Approximately how much is this in litres? _____

   1 mark

PS 4.   Joe tries to measure out the imperial measure of 1 stone. He has measured out 5 kilograms.

   Approximately how many more grams does he need to add? _____

   1 mark

Total: [   ] / 19 marks

Had a go [   ]   **Getting there** [   ]   **Got it!** [   ]

Perimeter, area and volume

- Measure and calculate the perimeter of composite rectilinear shapes
- Calculate and compare the area of rectangles
- Estimate volume of cuboids by counting cubes and capacity of objects

Perimeter

The **perimeter** of a shape is the length of the outside edge. It is usually measured in centimetres (cm) or metres (m).

Example

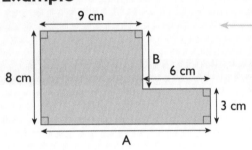

This **composite rectilinear shape** is made of two rectangles; the shape uses the right angle symbols. Opposite sides of a rectangle are equal.

There are missing sides:
- Side A = 9 cm + 6 cm = 15 cm
- Side B = 8 cm − 3 cm = 5 cm

Perimeter = 9 + 5 + 6 + 3 + 15 + 8 = 46
= **46 cm**

We can work out the lengths of the missing sides using the other measurements given in the diagram.

Area

The **area** of a shape is the amount of space inside a 2-D shape. It is measured using square units such as **square centimetres** (cm^2) or **square metres** (m^2).

Example

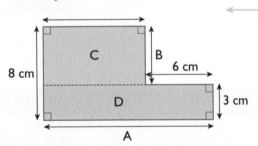

This composite rectilinear shape can be divided into two rectangles, C and D, as shown by the dashed line.

The area is calculated as
- Rectangle C = 9 cm × Side B
  = 9 × (8 − 3) = 9 × 5 = 45 cm^2
- Rectangle D = Side A × 3 cm
  = (9 + 6) × 3 = 15 × 3 = 45 cm^2
- Area of shape = 45 cm^2 + 45 cm^2
  = **90 cm^2**

Volume

The **volume** of a shape is the amount of space inside a 3-D shape. It is measured using cube units such as **cubic centimetres** (cm^3) or **cubic metres** (m^3).

Example

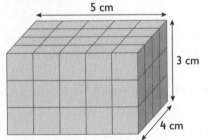

The volume of this cuboid is the space taken up by the whole shape.

One layer of cubes is 4 rows of 5 cubes and there are 3 layers.

4cm × 5cm × 3cm
= **60 cm^3**.

Capacity is another way of describing the space taken up by a 3-D object. It refers to how much liquid an object can hold in millilitres or litres. I cm^3 holds I ml; 1,000 cm^3 = I litre.

Challenge 1

1. a) Find the perimeter of this rectangle. _____

    b) Find the area of this rectangle. _____

    12 cm

    4 cm

    2 marks

2. a) What is the volume of this cube? _____

    4 cm

    4 cm

    4 cm

    b) Max makes a similar cube that is 3 cm long, 3 cm wide and 3 cm high.

    What is the volume of Max's cube? _____

    2 marks

Challenge 2

1. Find the perimeter and area of these shapes.

    a)

    10 cm

    12 cm

    15 cm

    5 cm

    b)

    15 cm

    5 cm

    8 cm

    10 cm

    Perimeter = _____   Area = _____

    Perimeter = _____   Area = _____

    4 marks

PS 2. Underline the rectangle with the largest area. Tick the rectangle with the smallest perimeter.

8 cm long, 7 cm wide

10 cm long, 2 cm wide

9 cm long, 6 cm wide

2 marks

Challenge 3

PS 1. Ned has a cubic container that measures 10 cm × 10 cm × 10 cm filled with water.

How many litres of water are in the container?   _____

1 mark

PS 2. a) Find the length of a square with an area of 196 cm². _____

    b) Find the length of a cube that has a volume of 125 cm³. _____

    2 marks

PS 3. The length of a rectangle is three times the width.

Find the length of the rectangle if the perimeter is 480 cm. _____

1 mark

Total: ☐ / 14 marks

Had a go ☐   **Getting there** ☐   **Got it!** ☐

Measurement word problems

- Solve measurement word problems

Solving word problems

When solving word problems, follow this sequence carefully:

1. Read the problem and decide what is being asked.
2. Look for the facts needed to answer the question.
3. Decide which **operation** or operations (addition, subtraction, multiplication, division or a combination of these) will be needed.
4. Complete the calculation.
5. Make sure the answer to the calculation answers the question asked.
6. Answer the question using the relevant **units**.
7. Check that the answer is reasonable and makes sense.

Example

Read this word problem:

Manisha went into a shop and bought a magazine.

How much change did she get?

Obviously, this question cannot be answered, because there is not enough information.

Now read this word problem:

Manisha went into a shop and bought a magazine that cost £5.85. She paid with a £20 note.

How much change did she get?

20 − 5.85 = 14.15

Answer: £14.15

Some word problems need two operations or more to be solved.

Example

Read this word problem:

Manisha went into a shop and bought a magazine that cost £5.85 and a newspaper for £2.75. She paid with a £20 note.

How much change did she get?

5.85 + 2.75 = 8.6

20 − 8.6 = 11.4

Answer: £11.40

Now read this word problem:

Manisha went into a shop and bought a magazine that cost £5.85 and a newspaper for £2.75. She has a £5 note, £2 coin and a 50p coin.

How much more money does she need?

5.85 + 2.75 = 8.6 ← First, find the total she needs to pay.

5 + 2 + 0.5 = 7.5 ← Second, find the total amount of money she has.

8.6 − 7.5 = 1.1 ← Finally, find the difference.

Answer: £1.10

Key words

- operation
- unit

Challenge 1

PS 1. Jan has two £20 notes that she uses to buy a train ticket for £27.35

How much change will she get? _____

1 mark

PS 2. Mo is running a cross-country race that is 3 kilometres long.

He has run 2,150 metres.

How much further has Mo left to run? _____

1 mark

PS 3. A bag of sweets has a mass of 0.45 kg.

What is the mass of 8 bags? _____

1 mark

PS 4. A teacher buys a 5-litre bottle of juice for a party.
She pours the drink into 20 glasses.

How many millilitres are in each glass? _____

1 mark

Challenge 2

PS 1. Leo buys three t-shirts that cost £17.95 each and a jumper for £27.50

How much does Leo spend altogether? _____

1 mark

PS 2. Maisie fits kitchen units. Two units are 600 mm wide and three are 450 mm wide.

What is the total length of the five units in metres? _____

1 mark

PS 3. Myra has a 3-kilogram bag of flour. She has used 700 g. She divides the rest into four bowls.

How much flour is in each bowl in grams? _____

1 mark

PS 4. A 2-litre bottle of juice can fill 5 glasses. Jay needs to fill 36 glasses.

How many 2-litre bottles will Jay need to buy?

1 mark

PS 5. Noah earns £18.75 for washing 3 cars.

How much will Noah earn for washing 9 cars? _____

1 mark

Challenge 3

PS 1. In a recipe, 3 eggs are used for every 400 g of flour. This makes 12 cupcakes.

a) How many eggs would be needed if 1.2 kg of flour were used?

b) How many cupcakes would be made?

2 marks

PS 2. Meena buys vegetables: 0.75 kg of parsnips, 300 g of carrots and 2 kg of potatoes.

a) What is the total mass of the vegetables? _____

b) With the fruit that Meena buys, the total mass of her shopping is 6.15 kg.

What is the mass of the fruit that Meena buys? _____

2 marks

PS 3. Harry needs to buy some wood for 7 shelves that are 75 cm long. The wood can be bought
in lengths of 2 metres. Shelves must be made in one single piece. Each length of wood costs £16.50

How much will Harry have to spend? _____

1 mark

Total: [ ] / 14 marks

| Had a go | Getting there | Got it! |

87

Progress test 4

1. **Write the missing numbers in these sequences.**

    a)   617,907   618,907   _____   620,907   621,907

    b)   121,588   _____   _____   121,888   121,988

2. **Write these Roman numerals as numbers.**

    a)   LIII = _____

    b)   CIX = _____

    c)   CDXLIV = _____

    d)   Which year is represented by the Roman numerals MCMXC?   _____

3. **Write the answers to these calculations.**

    a)   300 + 245 = _____   b)   68 + 69 = _____   c)   522 − 98 = _____

4. **Complete these calculations.**

    a)

    ```
        4  6  8  1
     -  1  9  7  9
    _____

    _____
    ```

    b)

    ```
        4  6  2  7
     +  5  3  8  7
    _____

    _____
    ```

5. **Write the answers to these calculations.**

    a)   60 × 8 = _____   b)   76 ÷ 4 = _____   c)   420 ÷ 7 = _____

6. **Complete the equivalent fractions.**

    a) $\dfrac{2}{5} = \dfrac{\boxed{}}{10} = \dfrac{6}{\boxed{}} = \dfrac{\boxed{}}{20} = \dfrac{10}{\boxed{}}$

    b) $\dfrac{3}{8} = \dfrac{15}{\boxed{}}$

    c) $\dfrac{5}{12} = \dfrac{\boxed{}}{48}$

7. **Write these decimal numbers as fractions.**

    a)   0.75 = _____   b)   0.3 = _____   c)   0.09 = _____

    Write these fractions as decimal numbers.

    d) $\dfrac{7}{10}$ = _____   e) $\dfrac{53}{100}$ = _____   f) $\dfrac{9}{1,000}$ = _____

PS 8.   **Rory has £60. He spends 25% of his money on cinema tickets.**

    a)   How much money does Rory spend on the cinema tickets?

    _____

    b)   His friend, Chen, only has 50% of the money Rory starts out with and spends 25% of his money on popcorn and drinks.

    How much money does Chen spend on popcorn and drinks?   _____

9. Convert these units of measure.

a) 700 cm = _____ metres

b) 800 g = _____ kilograms

c) 5,000 ml = _____ litres

3 marks

PS 10. This is a plan of Harvey's garden. What is the area of the garden?

30 m

5 m

_____

1 mark

11. Write these numbers in order, starting with the smallest.

54,865   53,856   53,568   54,368   53,865

_____   _____   _____   _____   _____

1 mark

12. Write a 5-digit number that has 4 ones, 7 hundreds and 2 tens of thousands.

_____

1 mark

13. Round 52,894 to the nearest:

a) ten _____   b) thousand _____   c) ten thousand _____

3 marks

PS 14. Anay collects 4,178 oranges from his orchard. 2,750 oranges are packed into boxes of 50 oranges and then 40 boxes are packed with 25 oranges.

How many oranges are left to be packed? _____

1 mark

15. a) What is the highest common factor of 27 and 36?

b) What is the lowest common multiple of 5 and 8?

2 marks

PS 16. The temperature in the freezer compartment is −17 °C. The temperature in the fridge is 3 °C.

What is the difference between the two temperatures? [ ] °C

1 mark

17. Complete these division calculations.

a) 4) 3 0 6 0   b) 8) 9 9 0 4

2 marks

PS 18. Usain Bolt is a sprinter. His fastest speed was calculated at 44.725 kilometres per hour.

a) What is this speed recorded to the 1st decimal place? _____

b) What is this speed recorded to the nearest whole number? _____

2 marks

PS 19. Kylie goes to the cinema. The film she wants to see lasts 175 minutes.

How long is this in hours and minutes? _____ hours _____ minutes

1 mark

PS 20. James lives on a farm. There is an old water tank that holds 100 gallons.

Approximately how many litres is this?

_____

1 mark

21. a) $8 - 10 - 2 =$ ☐   b) $-5 + 9 - 2 =$ ☐   c) $7 - 10 + 2 =$ ☐

3 marks

PS 22. Jonny earns £12.25 an hour.

a) How much will he earn if he works for 10 hours? _____

b) How much will he earn if he works for 100 hours? _____

2 marks

23. Complete these calculations.

a)
```
    5  2  8  6
 ×           6
 _____
```

b)
```
    3  0  7  8
 ×        3  7
 _____
```

2 marks

24. Write these fractions in order, starting with the smallest.

$\frac{1}{2}$ $\frac{2}{3}$ $\frac{7}{12}$ $\frac{5}{8}$ $\frac{13}{24}$

_____   _____   _____   _____   _____

1 mark

PS 25. Kelly and Jenny share £40. Kelly tells Jenny, "You can have a quarter of the money or 30% of the money."

What is the difference in the amount of money Jenny could get?

_____

1 mark

PS 26. A farmer wants to put a new fence around one of his fields. The rectangular field is 75 metres long and 60 metres wide. There is one gate that is 4 metres wide.

What is the length of fencing that the farmer will use?

_____

1 mark

PS 27. Leo completes this calculation in class:

6,734 – 2,984 = 3,750

He wants to check the calculation, so he uses an inverse calculation.

What is the inverse calculation Leo uses? _____

1 mark

28. a) $10^2 =$ _____   b) $9^3 =$ _____   c) $15^2 =$ _____

3 marks

PS 29. Penny uses some digital scales to measure out five similar amounts of flour.

Write the masses in order, starting with the lightest. The masses are:

0.696 kg   0.689 kg   0.703 kg   0.7 kg   0.69 kg

_____   _____   _____   _____   _____

1 mark

30. **Circle the numbers that are prime numbers.**

71 **72** **73** **75** **79**

1 mark

31. **A football club organises an away trip for 2,394 supporters. All the supporters on the away trip buy tickets from the club. The supporters are travelling by bus, train and car.**

The football club organises a special train with **684** seats. All the train seats are taken.

They organise 24 buses, each with 55 seats. All the bus seats are taken.

How many supporters travel by car? _____

1 mark

PS 32. **Hazel buys 8 pizzas for a party. She cuts the pizzas into eighths. At the end of the party $\frac{59}{8}$ have been eaten.**

How many pieces are left?

1 mark

PS 33. **Calculate the missing numerator in this calculation.**

$$\frac{3}{8} + \frac{\boxed{}}{24} + \frac{5}{6} = 1\frac{7}{24}$$

1 mark

PS 34. **The shaded face of this cuboid is 56 cm². The length of the cuboid is 15 cm.**

Area of shaded
face = 56 cm²

15 cm

What is the volume of the cuboid? _____

1 mark

PS 35. **Anna is buying a car. She checks how wide the car is and finds it is 1,785 mm wide. Anna also checks the width of her garage and finds it is 3.15 m wide.**

What is the amount of spare width?

_____

1 mark

PS 36. **Dev earns £25,000 a year. He is promoted at work and is given a 15% rise.**

How much extra will Dev earn a year?

_____

1 mark

PS 37. **Each day Petra drinks two bottles of water. Each bottle holds $\frac{11}{5}$ litres.**

How much water does Petra drink in a week?

_____

1 mark

PS 38. **An airline has different jumbo jets. They have a fleet of twenty-four that can carry 416 people and eighteen that can carry 524 people.**

If all the jumbo jets are in use, how many people could they carry?

_____

1 mark

Total: [ ] /71 marks

Relative clauses

- **Understand and use relative clauses**

Adapting, describing and modifying nouns

Relative clauses are used to add information about the noun, noun phrase or proper noun in a sentence – they are 'related' to the noun. A relative clause is a type of **subordinate clause**.

Relative clauses are introduced by a **relative pronoun**. These are: **who, whose, which, that. Where** and **when** are also sometimes used as relative pronouns.

Example

*The bike **that Molly rides** is very fast.*
The relative pronoun 'that' refers to 'the bike'.

> The relative clause describes 'the bike'.

*I went to visit my aunt **who will be 100 soon**.*
The relative pronoun 'who' refers to 'my aunt'.

> The relative clause describes 'my aunt'.

> The relative clause describes 'our neighbour'.

*Our neighbour, **whose house was burgled**, is having a new alarm.*
The relative pronoun 'whose' (the possessive form of 'who') refers to 'our neighbour'.

*The house **where Grandma was born** is very old.*
The relative pronoun 'where' refers to 'the house'.

> The relative clause describes 'the house'.

*The summer **when I was born** was beautiful.*
The relative pronoun 'when' refers to 'the summer'.

> The relative clause describes 'the summer'.

Embedded clauses

A relative clause can also be an **embedded clause**. An embedded clause is a subordinate clause in the middle of a sentence, usually separated with commas.

Example

The horse, **which I often ride**, is very strong.

> The relative clause describes the relationship with the very strong horse.

Sol, **who won the race**, was given a gold medal.

> The relative clause explains why Sol was given a gold medal.

In each of these sentences, the relative clause could be taken out; this would leave the main clause, which makes sense on its own. The relative clauses are also embedded clauses in these sentences.

1. Underline the relative clause in each sentence.

    a)   The car, that was old and noisy, stopped.

    b)   Gran, who plays golf each week, got a hole in one.

    c)   I have a big teddy, which I won in a raffle.

    d)   This is the painting that everyone is talking about.

    e)   There are the children who climbed over the fence.

5 marks

2. For each sentence above, write the preceding noun that each relative pronoun is related to.

    a) _____

    b) _____

    c) _____

    d) _____

    e) _____

5 marks

1. Circle the correct relative pronoun to use in each sentence.

    a)   Her brother, **who / that** joined the army, came home for Christmas.

    b)   She is the lady **whose / which** garden has all the gnomes.

    c)   We are going to the museum **where / which** has a lot of dinosaur bones.

    d)   This is the village **where / which** they live.

    e)   The house **that / where** my cousin lives in is in the city.

5 marks

1. Add a suitable relative clause to each sentence.

    a)   A nurse is a person _____

    _____

    b)   We are going to a beach _____

    _____

    c)   Cakes, _____,

    _____ contain lots of sugar.

    d)   The rain _____

    _____ was torrential.

    e)   Suddenly they heard a noise _____

    _____

5 marks

Total: ⬜ /20 marks

Had a go ⬜   **Getting there** ⬜   **Got it!** ⬜

93

Degrees of possibility

- Use adverbs and modal verbs to indicate degrees of possibility

Adverbs

Adverbs are used to modify (give more information about) **verbs**. They are words that can indicate time, place, manner or degree to which something was done (how much, how often or how well things were done).

Example

He went to school **yesterday**. | Indicates time.

We looked **everywhere**. | Indicates place.

I walked **slowly**. | Indicates manner.

The test was **extremely** hard. | Indicates degree.

Some adverbs indicate possibility.

Example

We will **definitely** visit the zoo. | **definitely** and **certainly** indicate things that are certain to happen.

You are **certainly** going to win now.

Surely it will be a nice day. | **surely** indicates it is expected but not definite.

They are **possibly** going to the museum.
Maybe it will rain.
Perhaps we can go to the beach. | **possibly**, **maybe** and **perhaps** indicate that events could happen but also have a chance of not doing so.

> **Remember**
>
> Adverbs can be used to indicate time, place, manner and degree.

> **Tip**
>
> When using modal verbs, think about the chances of something happening. If it is certain, use **can** or **will**. If it is not certain, use **might**, **may** or **could**.

Modal verbs

Modal verbs affect the meaning of other verbs in a sentence. They are also used to show the degree of possibility – whether something is certain (it will happen), probable (it most likely will happen) or possible (it might happen).

The modal verb always comes before the basic verb form, called the **infinitive**.

Example

It **might** <u>rain</u> later.
We **could** <u>take</u> an umbrella.
We **may** <u>get</u> on the boat now.
It **can** <u>be</u> cold on the lake.
You **must** <u>wear</u> a buoyancy aid.
The dog **would** <u>love</u> the water.
I **will** <u>steer</u> the boat.

> The infinitive form of the verb is underlined and the modal verb is shown in bold.

> **Key words**
>
> - adverb
> - verb
> - modal verb
> - infinitive

1. Underline the adverb in each sentence that shows the degree of possibility.

    a)   There is possibly a path through the forest.

    b)   Perhaps there is a café at the park.

    c)   She will surely make the best cake.

    d)   It's definitely going to snow later.

    4 marks

2. Look at the adverb in each sentence and tick the correct part of the table to show the degree of possibility indicated.

	Certain to happen	Not certain to happen
a) The Reds are certainly going to win now.		
b) Maybe you will find your coat on the playground.		
c) I will definitely have a milkshake to drink.		
d) We will possibly see whales on the boat trip.		

4 marks

1. Underline the modal verb in each sentence.

    a)   The water pooling on the floor meant there could be a leak in the new bathroom.

    b)   Jack said he would bake a cake for his teacher if he had time.

    c)   Liv was told she can have a day off school to go to her sister's wedding.

    d)   We must not be late home because we are going on holiday tomorrow.

    e)   The weather report said there might be snow at the weekend.

    f)   I should have gone straight home after school.

    6 marks

1. Choose four different suitable adverbs to indicate degree of possibility in the sentences below.

    a)   _____ we could go to visit them.

    b)   You will _____ wear a helmet when riding your bike.

    c)   It is _____ December because it is Christmas Day tomorrow.

    d)   _____ it will be sunny next time we visit.

    4 marks

2. Choose a suitable modal verb to complete each sentence.

    a)   You _____ decorate the cake with sweets.

    b)   They _____ wear their school uniform.

    c)   We _____ not touch the door because the paint is wet.

    d)   It _____ be home-time soon.

    4 marks

Total: [ ] /22 marks

Had a go [ ]   Getting there [ ]   Got it! [ ]

Verbs and verb tense

- **Recognise and understand the correct use of verb tense**

Verbs and tenses

Verbs are used to describe what is happening, what has happened or what will happen.

When the action happens is known as **tense**, and verb tenses can refer to things happening at different times – in the past, the present and the future.

- The **past** refers to something that has already happened.
- The **present** refers to something that is happening now.
- The **future** refers to something that has not happened yet but will do.

Example

I **am** tired. ← | simple present tense – I am tired right now

I **am** using my skateboard. ← | present progressive tense – I am doing it now

I **walked** home. ← | simple past tense – I walked home before now.

I **have read** a book. ← | present perfect tense – I have already done it

I **was cutting** the grass. ← | past progressive tense – I was doing it in the past

I **will talk** to the teacher. ← | future tense – I will do it in the future

Tense		Example
Present	Simple present	I eat
	Present progressive	I am eating
Past	Simple past	I ate
	Past progressive	I was eating
	Present perfect	I have eaten
Future	Simple future	I will eat
	Future progressive	I will be eating

Choosing the correct tense

If the incorrect verb tense is used, writing can become confusing for the reader and may lose its impact. Sentences will also be incorrect.

Example

- They **bought** an ice cream after they **swim** in the sea.

This sentence has two verbs – **bought** is the past tense of **buy** and **swim** is in the present tense. The two verbs need to agree:

- They **bought** an ice cream after they **swam** in the sea.

- She **will catch** the train to London and then **saw** a show.

The tense **will catch** is future, but **saw** is the past tense of **see**. The two verbs need to agree:

- She **will catch** a train to London and then **see** a show.

Challenge 1

1. Circle the correct form of the verb to complete each sentence.

   a) We **play / played** football in the garden last week.

   b) Everyone **jumped / jumping** on the bouncy castle when it was ready.

   c) She **works / working** hard to improve her running pace.

   d) He **ate / eats** breakfast before he gets dressed.

2. Rewrite each sentence from above but change the sentence so that it makes sense using the other form of each verb.

   a) _____

   _____

   b) _____

   _____

   c) _____

   _____

   d) _____

   _____

Challenge 2

1. Rewrite each sentence, ensuring that the two verbs have the same tense.

   a) He jumped over the wall and twists his ankle.

   _____

   _____

   b) She entered the competition and wins first prize.

   _____

   _____

   c) They walk along the path and arrived at a dead end.

   _____

   _____

Challenge 3

1. Think about a trip or holiday you would like to go on. Write three sentences about it, keeping the writing consistently in the future tense.

   _____

   _____

   _____

2. Rewrite the sentences from above in the past tense.

   _____

   _____

   _____

Total: [ ] / 17 marks

Had a go [ ]   **Getting there** [ ]   **Got it!** [ ]

Cohesion between sentences

- Build cohesion within paragraphs using adverbials of time to link sentences

Cohesion

It is important to make sure that there is **cohesion** between sentences in a paragraph. This means making the sentences link together well.

Adverbials of time (such as: after a while, later, the next day) are great devices to use for this purpose.

Example

Read this extract. This writing does not have cohesion.

> Sam stood on the rock. He jumped down onto the wet sand and stared at the sea. He started to walk along the shore. Sam noticed something grey in the water about 20 metres away.

Now read the same extract with improved cohesion.

> Sam stood on the rock. He **then** jumped down onto the wet sand and stared at the sea. **After a short while**, he started to walk along the shore. **At that moment**, Sam noticed something grey in the water about 20 metres away.

The sentences in this extract 'flow' much better – they follow on more fluently and each of the added words and phrases indicates when events happened. 'Soon' or 'eventually' could also be used instead of 'then'. 'Eventually', 'later' and 'sometime later' are alternatives that could replace 'after a short while'. 'Suddenly', 'soon' and 'a little later' are all ideas that could be used instead of 'at that moment'.

Other adverbials of time include:

- During the week
- Daily
- Later on
- Earlier that day
- After a few hours
- All of a sudden
- In a split second
- At that moment

Try to think of some more adverbials of time.

Remember

When writing, you should aim to engage the reader. This means that your writing needs to be interesting to read. Creating cohesion between sentences helps with this.

> The sentences simply state what Sam did. The writing is really just a list of sentences and it doesn't sound very interesting.

> The words in bold in the text below have been added to improve cohesion.

Tip

Try to use a range of adverbials in your writing to avoid repetition.

Tip

Adverbs are single words; adverbials tend to be groups of words.

Key words

- cohesion
- adverbial of time

98

1. Use the words below to create cohesion between the sentences and clauses.

   during   **before**   **then**   **at lunchtime**

   a) Jess went to school. _____ she had pizza.

   b) _____ Sam went out to play, he ate his lunch.

   c) First the children played chase, _____ they played with hoops.

   d) _____ the film, they ate lots of popcorn.

   4 marks

1. Underline the adverbs and adverbial phrases in the text which have been used to improve cohesion.

   Eden and Dev walked to the lake. Before long, they paddled in the water. Next, they started skimming stones. Eden was great at this because her mum had told her what to do.

   Later, they called Dev's dad to pick them up. After a few minutes, he arrived in his car.

   4 marks

2. Rewrite the last two sentences, of the above text, replacing the adverbs and adverbial phrases with alternative words.

   _____

   _____

   _____

   _____

   2 marks

1. Rewrite the following text, adding in adverbs and adverbial phrases, in the spaces shown, to improve cohesion.

   The car was dirty. During the journey, Dev said that it had not been cleaned for months. _____ Dev's dad had an idea. He told Eden and Dev they could clean the car. _____ they were home. _____ they could go inside, Dev's dad got out the bucket and hosepipe.

   _____

   _____

   _____

   _____

   _____

   _____

   4 marks

   Total: [   ] / 14 marks

   Had a go [   ]   **Getting there** [   ]   **Got it!** [   ]

Cohesion between paragraphs

- Build cohesion across paragraphs

Linking paragraphs

Paragraphs organise writing and make it easier to read and understand. However, as with sentences, the flow of the writing can be much improved if there is **cohesion** between paragraphs. This means giving a sense of how each paragraph follows on from the previous one.

Using **fronted adverbials** (often followed by a comma), **adverbials of time** and **adverbials of place** in your writing creates cohesion by adding further detail.

Example

Read this extract. This writing does not have cohesion.

> Gina heard a strange noise behind the tent. She ran.
>
> She climbed over the fence, crossed the garden, and entered the house. The door slammed behind her and the young girl fell to the floor sobbing.
>
> Her mum rushed to her side, a little panicked by Gina's tears. Gina told her about the noise. Mum explained that Gina's brother had gone out to the tent. Gina said that she did not find it funny and would not go back out to the tent again.

Now read this version of the same extract. This writing shows improved cohesion.

> **Before it went dark**, Gina heard a strange noise behind the tent. **Immediately**, she ran **towards her home**.
>
> **As fast as she could**, she climbed over the fence, crossed the garden, and entered the house. The door slammed behind her and the young girl fell to the floor sobbing.
>
> **Straight away**, her mum rushed to her side, a little panicked by Gina's tears. Gina told her about the noise. Mum explained that Gina's brother had gone out to the tent **to play a trick**. Gina said that she did not find it funny and would not go back out to the tent again.

Remember

When planning your writing, make sure that paragraphs are in a logical order to help them follow on from each other.

Remember

A fronted adverbial is any adverb or adverbial that comes at the beginning of the sentence, before the verb.

The writing is really just a list of sentences and paragraphs and so it doesn't sound very interesting.

Adverbials have been added at the beginning and end of some paragraphs. These create greater cohesion between the paragraphs by giving more detail about actions, time and place.

Key words

- paragraph
- cohesion
- fronted adverbial
- adverbial of time
- adverbial of place

1. Choose an adverbial of time for the opening sentence of each paragraph from a recount of a school trip to a farm. Write it in the space provided.

During the afternoon   **First**   **Before lunch**   **Later on**   **Next**

a) _____ , we were told where to leave our bags and the farmer showed us where the toilets were.

b) _____ , three groups went to the lambing shed and three groups went to see the horses.

c) _____ , everybody had to wash their hands.

d) _____ , we all had chance to feed baby animals.

e) _____ , it was time to go home.

5 marks

1. Read the text below and then choose the most suitable place to add each adverbial phrase to improve cohesion.

inside the house   **after the downpour**   **soon**   **quickly**   **later on**

Suki walked along the road _____. It felt a long way home on a dark December evening.

She was wet and cold _____.

_____ her dad handed her a towel and gave her a warm hug. Suki was worn out and needed to rest her tired feet.

_____ she was dry and lay down on the settee.

_____ Suki was feeling better and decided to make everyone some supper.

5 marks

1. Add a suitable adverb or adverbial phrase to each space to improve cohesion between paragraphs.

They could see land ahead, the shapes of hills silhouetted by the setting sun – black hills against a pink sky.

_____ they could see more details. The lights from coastal towns and villages started to shine and reflect from the sea.

_____ the boat approached the lights. The battered vessel could not be rushed.

_____ the bedraggled crew were becoming excited. Land would mean fresh water, fruit and meat.

_____ the boat managed to dock.

4 marks

Total: _____ / 14 marks

Had a go ☐   **Getting there** ☐   **Got it!** ☐

Commas to clarify meaning

- Use commas to clarify meaning and avoid ambiguity

Ambiguity

Ambiguity is when something is not quite clear. If writing is ambiguous, this can cause confusion to the reader.

Using commas to clarify meaning

To avoid ambiguity, **commas** can be used to clarify the intended meaning.

Example

"Time to eat children," called Mum.

Does this really mean Mum is going to eat children? Let's hope not. Of course, Mum is probably telling the children that it is time to eat. So, a comma is needed here to remove the ambiguity.

"Time to eat, children," called Mum.

The comma removes the ambiguity by separating the information 'time to eat' from the word 'children'. This shows that mum was addressing the children.

Bella likes cooking her friends and her cats.

A comma is needed in the above sentence unless we really do mean that Bella cooks her friends and cats!

Bella likes cooking, her friends and her cats.

The commas remove the ambiguity as it is now clear that this is a list of things that Bella likes.

Commas in lists

The example above shows how commas can also be used to separate items in a list. In the list of things that Bella likes, there are three items: cooking, her friends and cats.

It is important when using commas to separate items in a list that a comma is placed after each item apart from the next to last item (which is usually followed by 'and' or 'or') and the last item.

Example

Darcy decided to have cheese, onion, pepper, ham and mushrooms on her pizza.

Ed could not decide whether to have pasta, pizza, a sandwich or a salad.

Suhaib's salad contained lettuce, avocado, tomatoes, cucumber, spring onions and cheese.

1. Add a comma in the correct place in the sentences.

   a) Tilly had pizza chips and milkshake at the party.

   b) The children played ball skipping and hopping games.

   c) It was Kenji's birthday and he had cakes ice cream and jelly for tea.

   d) Stella enjoyed reading writing and picture books.

   4 marks

2. Write lists of four items to complete each sentence below.

   a) They knew her name was either _____

   _____

   b) Your lessons this week are _____

   _____

   c) From the shops, we need _____

   _____

   d) Some countries I would like to visit are _____

   _____

   4 marks

1. Rewrite each sentence, using a comma to remove any ambiguity.

   a) "Hurry up and hide Jack," said Lisa.

   _____

   b) "Can we bake Grandma?" asked the children.

   _____

   c) Most of the time travellers take a taxi from the airport.

   _____

   d) Sam likes his friends playing computer games and football.

   _____

   4 marks

1. For each of the examples in Challenge 2, write a short explanation of why a comma is needed in each.

   a) _____

   _____

   b) _____

   _____

   c) _____

   _____

   d) _____

   _____

   4 marks

   Total: ☐ / 16 marks

   Had a go ☐   **Getting there** ☐   **Got it!** ☐

Parenthesis

- **Use brackets, dashes or commas to indicate parenthesis**

What is parenthesis?

Parenthesis is a word, phrase or clause inserted into a sentence as an afterthought, to give extra information or to clarify a point.

If the parenthesis is removed, what is left still makes sense.

Example

Pep and Fran are coming to visit next week.

This sentence is grammatically correct.

It could also have further information added, such as who Pep and Fran are. This extra information would be added as parenthesis.

Parenthesis is indicated by **brackets**, **commas** or **dashes**.

Example

Pep and Fran (our friends from Spain) are coming to visit next week.

This additional information is placed in brackets immediately after the part of the sentence that it is providing information about.

If the words in brackets are removed, the sentence about Pep and Fran coming to visit still makes sense.

Example

Pep and Fran, who are our friends from Spain, are coming to visit next week.

Here, the words in parentheses are a **relative clause**, shown by commas.

Again, removal of the words between the commas will leave a grammatically correct sentence.

A relative clause is a group of words that adds information about the noun(s) in the sentence, but cannot stand alone as a sentence.

Example

Pep and Fran – our lovely friends from sunny Spain – are coming to visit next week.

Here, the words in parentheses are shown by dashes.

The choice of punctuation used to show parenthesis is largely up to the writer's personal preference. The main thing is that they are used correctly.

> **Remember**
>
> If you remove the parenthesis, the remaining words must still make sense.

> **Tip**
>
> There is no set rule for using commas, brackets or dashes for parenthesis. You just need to go with what feels right.

> **Key words**
>
> - parenthesis/parentheses
> - brackets
> - comma
> - dash
> - relative clause

Challenge 1

1. Insert brackets into the correct place in each sentence.

   a) My sisters both netball players go to college.

   b) The team played really well scoring two goals and won the game.

   c) We ordered a lot from the takeaway we were really hungry!

   d) Betty and Jim from London won the contest.

2. Underline the relative clause in each sentence.

   a) The house that has just been built is enormous.

   b) Roisin had a pony that had a long mane.

   c) The old man who works in the shop is very kind.

   d) The test that I spent hours revising for was cancelled.

Challenge 2

1. Insert commas to show the relative clause in each sentence.

   a) Jenny's parents who are doctors work at the hospital.

   b) The car which won the race last year is up for sale.

   c) Kelly who plays for the rugby team got a medal for good training.

   d) Danny's grandad who writes stories was on television.

2. Indicate whether you think each sentence uses parentheses correctly or not with a tick (✓) or a cross (✗).

   a) They dressed for summer – shorts, hats, sunglasses – even though it was still the middle of winter.

   b) The traffic, usually busy at this time was, moving well.

   c) Rosie the (best dancer) in the class was amazing.

   d) The sun, rising into a clear sky, was already warm.

   e) Evan – stylish – and chatty as ever made everybody laugh.

Challenge 3

1. Rewrite each incorrect sentence from Challenge 2, question 2 above, using the given parentheses in the correct places.

   _____

   _____

   _____

   _____

   _____

   _____

Total: ____ /20 marks

Had a go ☐   **Getting there** ☐   **Got it!** ☐

Progress test 5

1. Underline the prefix or suffix in each word, then use the word in a sentence.

   a) careful

   _____

   _____

   b) reappear

   _____

   _____

   c) dislike

   _____

   _____

   d) slowly

   _____

   _____

   4 marks

2. Add a comma in the correct place in each sentence.

   a) On the trip were Ben Naz and Jess.

   b) We ate cheese crisps and chicken nuggets at the party.

   c) Milly's three hobbies are painting sailing boats and swimming.

   d) Everyone heard the fizz whoosh and bang of the firework.

   4 marks

3. Complete each sentence to make a simile.

   a) He crawled along _____

   b) Her angry stare was _____

   c) The paper drifted into the sky _____

   d) The variety of food was colourful _____

   4 marks

4. Change each word below into a verb by adding -ise, -ate, -en or -ify.

   a) wide_____

   b) just_____

   c) medic_____

   d) real_____

   e) solid_____

   f) hard_____

   g) alien_____

   h) class_____

   8 marks

5. Replace the underlined words and phrases with more effective descriptions.

   a) The sea was <u>rough</u>.

   _____

   _____

   b) Overhead there were <u>clouds</u>.

   _____

   _____

   c) Their small boat was <u>bobbing</u> up and down.

   _____

   _____

3 marks

6. Underline the relative clause in each sentence.

   a) Ciara's new ball that bounces really high was a present from Tom.

   b) Seb, who goes to gym club, can do somersaults.

   c) Ged has a dog, which he walks twice a day.

   d) The new house where James lives is very nice.

4 marks

7. Choose a suitable modal verb to complete each sentence.

   a) They _____ reach the roof so they needed a ladder.

   b) We _____ leave for school at 8am.

   c) Mum told us that we _____ have pasta for tea.

   d) When crossing the road, they _____ be very careful.

4 marks

8. Rewrite each sentence, ensuring that the two highlighted verbs are written in the past tense.

   a) Kelly **smile** and then **eat** all the ice cream.

   _____

   _____

   b) We **play** netball and **win**.

   _____

   _____

   c) They **run** fast and **finish** first in the relay race.

   _____

   _____

   d) She **draw** a picture and **show** it to Mum.

   _____

   _____

e) He **dance** at the disco and **have** a great time.

_____

_____

f) Milly **bake** a cake and **sell** it to her gran.

_____

_____

6 marks

9. Insert brackets in the correct place in each sentence.

a) Henry VIII an English king had six wives.

b) We went to Paris the capital of France for the weekend.

c) The house probably haunted had been in their family for centuries.

d) Ella and Jack my cousins won the singing competition.

4 marks

10. Read the passage below.

> Joe knew his way through the dead trees, slipping under and beyond burnt branches, brambles and bush. It had never been the same since the fire. He remembered the crackle of flames as the trees caught light. He remembered the smoke and he remembered the ash the next day – a blanket over everything. The ash had long since washed away and now old Joe crept around, cunning as a fox, seeking out any new shoots, any living creatures, in fact anything that would show him life was returning to the woodland. Anything to provide hope.

a) Identify four examples of figurative language from the passage. Write the phrase or sentence for each and label it with the name of the figurative device used.

Example	Device
_____	_____
_____	_____
_____	_____
_____	_____

8 marks

b) In the passage, what do you think the words 'Anything to provide hope' mean?

_____

_____

_____

1 mark

11. State whether each of these sentences is fact or opinion.

a) The garden looks better than ever. _____

b) We moved house two years ago. _____

c) It's amazing that so many people like that film. _____

d) I have the best friends in the world. _____

e)   Half of the teachers at my school don't drive. _____

f)   It's quicker for me to walk to school than to get the bus. _____

6 marks

12. **Circle the correct spelling of the words to complete each sentence.**

a)   I was **ancious / anxious** about taking my driving test.

b)   It's **official / offisial**: I will be a teenager next week.

c)   He is still **infexious / infectious** until the spots have scabbed over.

d)   There is a **partial / parcial** closure to the school while repairs are being done.

4 marks

13. **Read the poem and then answer the questions.**

> Deep in the jungle live the animals and trees
> With the rain and sunshine and the gentle breeze,
> And if you listen carefully
> you might just hear,
> strange, musical, animal sounds, quiet but clear…
>
> Creatures of the jungle came from all around
> to see what was making such a splendid sound.
> They smiled and danced
> and clapped their hands
> for the amazing new musical jungle band.

a)   Explain what sort of voice you think this poem should be read with.

_____

b)   What word rhymes with 'breeze'?

_____

c)   What word is used in the poem to mean 'peculiar'?

_____

d)   Give an example of alliteration from the poem.

_____

e)   Who would the audience be for this poem?

_____

5 marks

14. **Underline the silent letter in each word below and then write a sentence containing that word.**

a)   knowledge

_____

b)   calf

_____

c)   comb

_____

d)   wrong

_____

4 marks

Total: [ ] /69 marks

2-D shapes

- Use properties of rectangles to deduce related facts
- Find missing lengths and angles of rectangles
- Distinguish between regular and irregular polygons

Properties of rectangles

A **rectangle** is a **2-D** shape; it is a **quadrilateral** (four-sided shape). A rectangle has:

- 2 pairs of equal and **parallel** sides
- 4 right angles
- 2 equal **diagonals**
- diagonals that bisect (cross over) each other.

A **square** is also a 2-D shape. It is a type of rectangle and has the same properties, but its four sides are equal length.

Finding missing lengths and angles of rectangles

Opposite sides of a rectangle are equal, so if one side is known, then its opposite side is known. The other missing sides can only be found if the **perimeter** or **area** of the rectangle is known.

Example

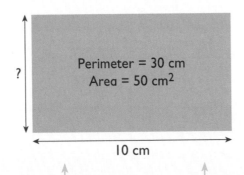

Perimeter = 30 cm
Area = 50 cm²

?

10 cm

> Two opposite sides have a total of 20 cm, and we are told that the perimeter is 30 cm.
>
> 30 − 20 = 10
>
> This means the other two sides total 10 cm so 10 ÷ 2 = 5
>
> The missing length is 5 cm.

> We are told that the area is 50 cm².
>
> The area is the length multiplied by the width, so if we do the inverse we get:
>
> 50 ÷ 10 = 5
>
> The missing length is 5 cm.

All angles of a rectangle and a square are right angles (90°). A diagonal may split the angle of a rectangle or square in two, but they will always total 90°. Opposite triangles formed by sides and diagonals are identical.

Regular and irregular polygons

A **regular** 2-D **polygon** must have equal sides and equal angles. Any 2-D shape that does not have equal sides and equal angles is **irregular**.

A square is a rectangle and is always regular – it has four equal sides and four right angles. But not all rectangles are regular: some are **oblong** and are irregular, because although they have equal angles, not all four sides are equal.

Remember

Learning the properties of each shape will help you find missing lengths and angles accurately.

Remember

All angles of a rectangle and a square are right angles (90°).

Remember

A polygon is any 2-D shape with three or more straight sides.

Key words

- rectangle
- 2-D
- quadrilateral
- parallel
- diagonal
- square
- perimeter
- area
- regular
- polygon
- irregular
- oblong

1. Find the length of the missing sides of these rectangles.

a)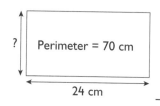
? Perimeter = 70 cm

24 cm _____

b)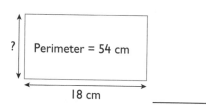
? Perimeter = 54 cm

18 cm _____

2 marks

2. Find the length of the missing sides of these rectangles.

a)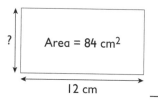
? Area = 84 cm²

12 cm _____

b)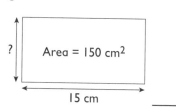
? Area = 150 cm²

15 cm _____

2 marks

3. Circle the irregular shape.

1 mark

Challenge 2

1. Complete the table of measurements of rectangles to show the lengths of the missing sides.

	Length	Width	Perimeter
a)	35 cm	_____	90 cm
b)	_____	22 cm	120 cm
c)	74 cm	_____	200 cm

	Length	Width	Area
d)	_____	5 cm	75 cm²
e)	14 cm	_____	98 cm²
f)	_____	12 cm	240 cm²

6 marks

Challenge 3

1. Complete the table of measurements of rectangles to show the lengths of the missing sides.

	Length	Width	Perimeter
a)	14 cm	_____	39 cm
b)	123 cm	_____	390 cm
c)	174 cm	_____	405 cm

	Length	Width	Area
d)	25 cm	_____	175 cm²
e)	45 cm	_____	900 cm²
f)	_____	20 cm	3600 cm²

6 marks

2. Sam says, "A rhombus has 4 equal sides, so it is regular." Explain why Sam is incorrect.

_____

_____

1 mark

Total: [   ] / 18 marks

Had a go [ ]   Getting there [ ]   Got it! [ ]

3-D shapes

- Recognise a range of 3-D shapes
- Identify 3-D shapes from 2-D representations

3-D shapes

3-D shapes are solid shapes. They are usually described as having a **length**, **width** (or breadth) and **height**. Some 3-D shapes have special properties and names.

The properties include the number of faces (flat sides), edges (lines that join two faces) and **vertices** (corners where three or more straight edges meet or where a curved face forms a point).

A cuboid has 6 faces (three pairs of faces that are parallel to each other), 12 edges and 8 vertices.

A cube is a special kind of cuboid with equal lengths, widths and heights. The faces of a cube are all squares.

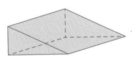

A prism has two identical end faces; the other faces are rectangles. The end faces can be any 2-D shape and the shape gives the prism its name, e.g. triangular prism.

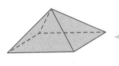

A pyramid has a base. The edges of the vertices of the base meet at an apex (a point that is furthest from the base). The base gives the pyramid its name, e.g. square-based pyramid.

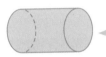

A cylinder has three faces – two end faces that are circles and a curved face.

A cone has two faces – a circular base and a curved face that forms an **apex**.

2-D representations of 3-D shapes

All the shapes shown above are 2-D representations of 3-D shapes. The dotted lines are the edges that could not be seen if the shape were not transparent.

Example

Here are two representations of a cube:

Here the dotted lines are the edges seen though the cube.

Here it is drawn as a solid, so not all the edges can be seen.

Challenge 1

1. Name these 3-D shapes.

   a) _____

   b) _____

   c) _____

   3 marks

PS 2. Complete these facts about 3-D shapes.

   a) A cube has ☐ faces.

   b) A triangular prism has ☐ faces.

   c) A pentagonal-based pyramid has ☐ faces.

   3 marks

Challenge 2

1. Name these 3-D shapes.

   a) _____

   b) _____

   c) _____

   3 marks

PS 2. Name these 3-D shapes.

   a) This shape is a prism. It has 5 faces, 9 edges and 6 vertices.

   What type of prism is it? _____

   b) This shape is a pyramid. It has 7 faces, 12 edges and 7 vertices.

   What type of pyramid is it? _____

   2 marks

Challenge 3

1. These shapes are made from cubes. How many faces, edges and vertices do they have?

   a) faces ☐

   edges ☐

   vertices ☐

   b) faces ☐

   edges ☐

   vertices ☐

   6 marks

2. Here is a shape made from 6 cubes.

   Draw the shape on squared paper as if you were looking at it from:

   a) the top view

   b) the side view

   c) the front view

   the top view

   the side view

   the front view

   3 marks

Total: ☐ /20 marks

Had a go ☐   **Getting there** ☐   **Got it!** ☐

Angles

- Know that angles are measured in degrees, and compare acute, obtuse and reflex angles
- Identify angles at a point, on a straight line or as part of a right angle

Angles

An **angle** is a measure of turn. Angles are measured in **degrees**, e.g. 24 degrees is recorded as 24°. There are 360° in one full turn.

Example

Arrow 1 has turned to point in the same direction of Arrow 2.

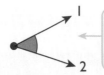

The turn is shown by the blue area with the curved edge showing the turn.

Some angles have special names. A right angle is shown by a symbol: a small square.

an **acute**
angle –
less than 90°

a **right angle,**
90° –
a quarter turn

an **obtuse angle**
– more than 90°
and less than
180°

a **straight**
angle, 180° –
a half turn

a **reflex angle**
– more than
180°

Remember

When deciding whether an angle is acute, obtuse or reflex, compare them with right angles and a straight angle.

Calculating angles

It is possible to find missing angles by calculating from known facts, such as that a right angle = 90° and a straight angle = 180°.

Example

A right angle is shown with two angles. One of the angles is 57°.
What is the second angle?

We know that a right angle is 90° so:
90 – 57 = 33
So the second angle is **33°**

Two angles form a full turn. One of the angles is 208°.
What is the second angle?

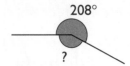

We know that a full turn is 360° so:
360 – 208 = 152
So the second angle is **152°**

Remember

When finding missing angles, calculate from known facts, such as a straight angle is 180°

Key words

- angle
- degrees
- acute angle
- right angle
- obtuse angle
- straight angle
- reflex angle

Challenge 1

1. Each angle has a letter, A to E. Write the letters to show the order of the angles from smallest to largest.

A   B   C   D   E

_____ _____ _____ _____ _____

1 mark

2. Here are five angles. Tick the acute angles.

1 mark

Challenge 2

1. Circle the obtuse angles.

88°   **178°**   **200°**   **98°**   **21°**   **359°**

1 mark

2. Find the missing angles on these straight lines.

a)

128°
?

b)

?   87°

2 marks

3. These angles all show a full turn. Find the missing angles.

a)

338°
?

b)

167°
?

2 marks

Challenge 3

1. Find the missing angles.

a)

189°
?

b)

36°   71°
?

2 marks

2. A right angle is divided equally into 4 angles. What size is each angle?

1 mark

3. 35°, 86° and a third angle make a straight angle. What is the third angle?

1 mark

4. Jay says, "If you add an acute angle to an obtuse angle, you always make a reflex angle."

Explain why Jay is incorrect.

_____

_____

1 mark

Total: ☐ / 12 marks

Had a go ☐   **Getting there** ☐   **Got it!** ☐

Reflection

- **Identify, describe and represent the position of a shape following a reflection**

Reflecting shapes

A **reflection** of a shape is to view the shape as it would be seen in a mirror.

Example

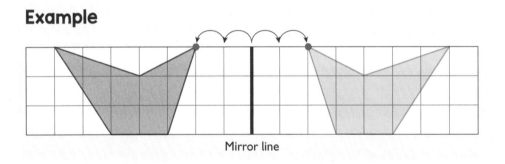

Mirror line

> The **mirror line** is the line of reflection. This is the line over which the shape must be 'flipped' so it appears as a reflection on the other side of the mirror line.

Although the shape is flipped and will appear the other way round, it stays the same shape and the same size. The shape, including each **vertex**, must also stay the same distance from the mirror line.

Example

Mirror line

> **Tip**
>
> A good way to draw the reflected shape is to focus on the vertices of the shape. Each vertex needs to be the same distance from the mirror line. Then join the vertices to form the sides. See the example alongside where the vertex shown by the red dot is two squares from the mirror line.

The mirror line does not have to be vertical. Horizontal and diagonal lines may be used.

Example

The shapes are reflections of each other.

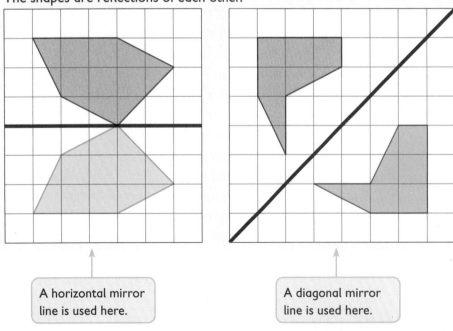

A horizontal mirror line is used here.

A diagonal mirror line is used here.

Key words

- reflection
- mirror line
- vertex

Challenge 1

1. Tick the lower shape that is a reflection of the shape above it.

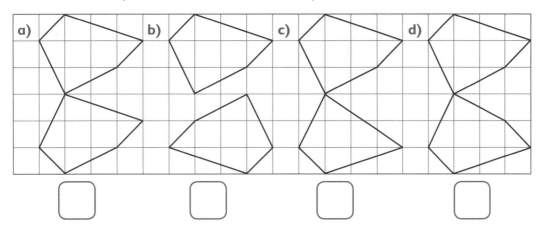

a) ☐   b) ☐   c) ☐   d) ☐

☐ 1 mark

2. Draw reflections of the four shapes. Look at the position of the mirror line.

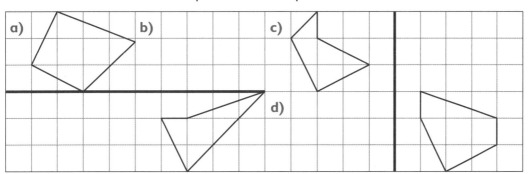

a)   b)   c)   d)

☐ 4 marks

Challenge 2

1. Draw reflections of the three shapes.

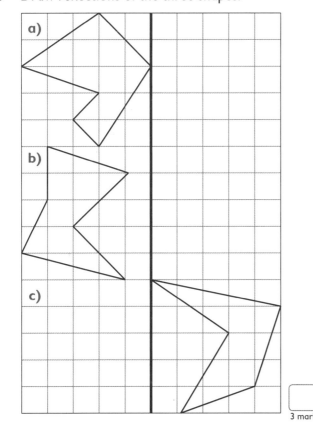

a)

b)

c)

☐ 3 marks

Challenge 3

1. Draw reflections of the three shapes.

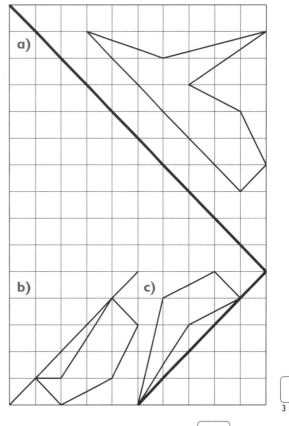

a)

b)   c)

☐ 3 marks

Total: ☐ / 11 marks

Had a go ☐   **Getting there** ☐   **Got it!** ☐

Translation

- Identify, describe and represent the position of a shape following a translation

Translating shapes

A **translation** of a shape means to 'slide' a shape horizontally or vertically. As the shape moves, it remains the same size and stays in the same orientation.

Example

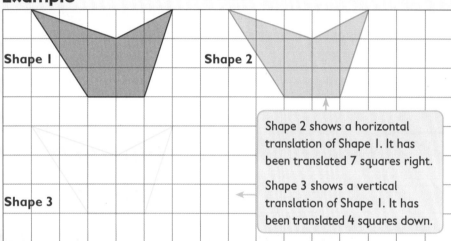

Shape 2 shows a horizontal translation of Shape 1. It has been translated 7 squares right.

Shape 3 shows a vertical translation of Shape 1. It has been translated 4 squares down.

Shapes can appear to have been translated diagonally, but this is two translations: one horizontally and one vertically. The horizontal translation is always given first. Sometimes the translated shape overlaps its original position.

Example

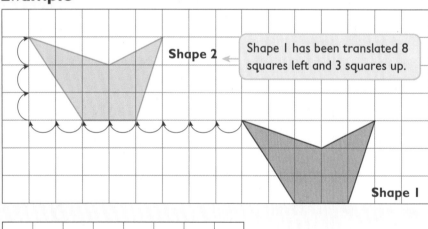

Shape 1 has been translated 8 squares left and 3 squares up.

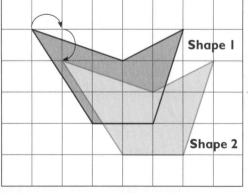

Shape 1 is translated 1 square right and 1 square down.

Key words

- translation
- vertices

1. Draw the shape in the translated positions. Translate each shape from the original.

   a) 3 squares left, 2 squares up   **b)** 2 squares right, 1 square down

   c) 8 squares right, 3 squares up **d)** 6 squares left, 3 squares down

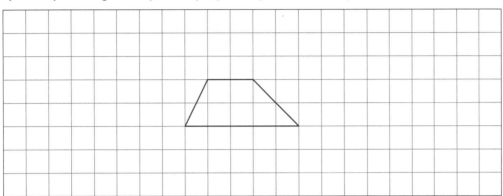

4 marks

1. Parallelograms (P) are drawn on the grid. Describe the translations of:

   a) P 1 to P 3 _____

   b) P 2 to P 5 _____

   c) P 5 to P 1 _____

   d) P 4 to P 2 _____

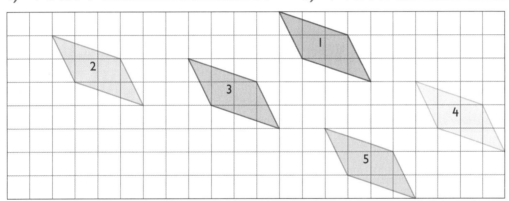

4 marks

1. This is part of a coordinate grid. A square is drawn on the grid at coordinates (10, 8), (10, 12), (14, 8) and (14, 12)

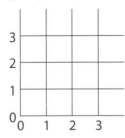

   What would the coordinates of the square be if the square were translated as follows:

   a) 3 squares left and 4 squares up? _____

   _____

   b) 5 squares right and 2 squares down? _____

   _____

   c) 1 square left and 5 squares down? _____

   _____

   d) 2 squares right and 6 squares up? _____

   _____

   4 marks

   Total: ____ / 12 marks

Had a go ☐   **Getting there** ☐   **Got it!** ☐

119

Tables and timetables

- Complete, read and interpret information in tables and timetables

Tables

Tables display information. Interpreting the information involves reading the categories shown in the table.

Example

This table gives information about a Fitness Club.

Age of Members	Under 18 years	18–30 years	31–50 years	Over 50 years
Men	26	64	86	34
Women	18	72	64	47

How many members of the Fitness Club are aged over 30?

To answer this question, look at the columns giving the number of members aged 31–50 years and over 50 years, along with both rows for these columns.

86 + 64 + 34 + 47 = 231, so **231** members are aged over 30

Frequency tables are used to collect information. They involve keeping a tally then recording the results.

Example

Create a frequency table to show the age groups of the club members who attend on one day.

Age groups				
24	31	16	22	52
27	55	17	15	41
34	21	27	41	19
41	22	31	26	53

Tally		Total
Under 18 years	|||	3
18–30 years	⸽⸽⸽⸽ |||	8
31–50 years	⸽⸽⸽⸽		6
Over 50 years	|||	3

The table is completed by recording a tally of the age groups, totalling the tally and recording in the frequency table.

Tip

Look at all the information given in a table, including the column and/or row titles.

Timetables

Timetables are used to order a sequence of events, e.g. class timetables, listings for television programmes, bus and train timetables.

Here is part of a train timetable for trains from York to Newcastle.

York	09:45	10:18	10:51	11:18	11:45
Northallerton		10:31		11:31	
Darlington	10:16	10:48	11:22	11:50	12:16
Durham	10:33	11:04		12:05	12:33
Newcastle	10:45	11:16	11:54	12:17	12:45

The timetable shows what time the train leaves each station. An empty cell means the train does not stop at that station.

Key word

- frequency table

Use these tables to answer all the questions.

This is a train timetable.

York	09:45	10:18	10:51	11:18
Northallerton		10:31		11:31
Darlington	10:16	10:48	11:22	11:50
Durham	10:33	11:04		12:05
Newcastle	10:45	11:16	11:54	12:17

This table shows passengers on trains from York. Some numbers in the table are missing.

	Train leaving York at:				
	09:45	10:18	10:51	11:18	Total
Men	256	198	148	142	
Women	187	194		146	679
Children	27	34			125
Total		426	336	316	1548

Challenge 1

PS 1. How long does the 10:18 train from York take to reach Newcastle? _____ ☐ 1 mark

PS 2. If the 09:45 train leaves on time, where will it be after 48 minutes? _____ ☐ 1 mark

PS 3. Which train is the fastest from York to Darlington? _____ ☐ 1 mark

PS 4. How many men travel on the four trains from York? _____ ☐ 1 mark

Challenge 2

PS 1. Toby arrives at York Station at 5 minutes to 10.
How long will he have to wait for the next train to Newcastle? _____ ☐ 1 mark

PS 2. Layla catches the 11:18 train from York to travel to Darlington.
The train leaves 3 minutes late but arrives 1 minute early.

How long does the journey take? _____ ☐ 1 mark

PS 3. A train leaves York at 11:45 and follows the same timetable as the 09:45 train from York.
At what time will the train arrive in Newcastle? _____ ☐ 1 mark

PS 4. How many women are on the 10:51 train from York? _____ ☐ 1 mark

Challenge 3

PS 1. Maxine arrives at York Station at 20 minutes to 11.
How long will she have to wait for the next train to Durham? _____ ☐ 1 mark

PS 2. Jan leaves home at 10:45, catches the 11:18 train from York, arrives in Newcastle and gets to the office for a meeting 20 minutes later.
How long does it take Jan to travel from her home to the office? _____ ☐ 1 mark

PS 3. How many children are on the 10:51 train from York? _____ ☐ 1 mark

PS 4. Sam says, '426 people left on the 10:18 train from York, so 426 people must have arrived in Newcastle.'
Explain why Sam could be incorrect. _____

_____ ☐ 1 mark

Total: ☐ / 12 marks

Had a go ☐   **Getting there** ☐   **Got it!** ☐

Graphs

- Solve comparison, sum and difference problems using information in a line graph

Line graphs

A **line graph** is a graph with a line (or lines) that displays continuous information, often over a period of time.

Example

This line graph gives the temperature from 6:00 a.m. to 8:00 p.m. over one day. The temperatures are plotted at 2-hourly intervals.

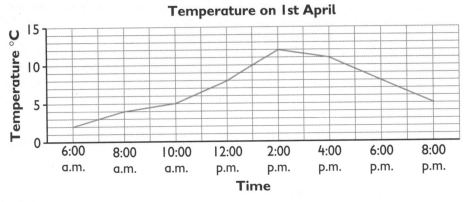

The line shows how the temperature rises and falls through the day.

The only certain temperatures are those that were recorded at 2-hourly intervals. The times in between are estimated temperatures, e.g. the temperature at 6:00 a.m. is 2 °C but at 7:00 a.m. is likely to be 3 °C.

Line graphs can have more than one line.

Example

This graph shows temperatures inside and outside for one day.

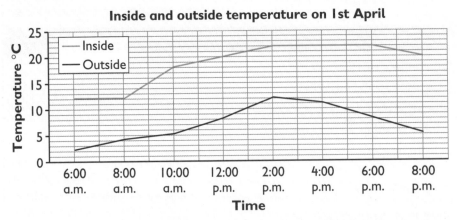

We can compare the temperature along one line or between the two lines:

What is the difference between the outside and inside temperatures at 8:00 p.m.?

Answer: 15 °C ← Outside is 5°C and inside in 20°C so 20 − 5

What is the difference between the inside temperature at 6:00 a.m. and 6:00 p.m.?

Answer: 10 °C ← At 6:00 a.m. is 12°C and at 6:00 p.m. is 22°C so 22 − 12

Key word

- line graph

Use this line graph to answer all the questions.

This line graph shows the mass of two babies during the first year after they were born. The masses were recorded on the first day of each month.

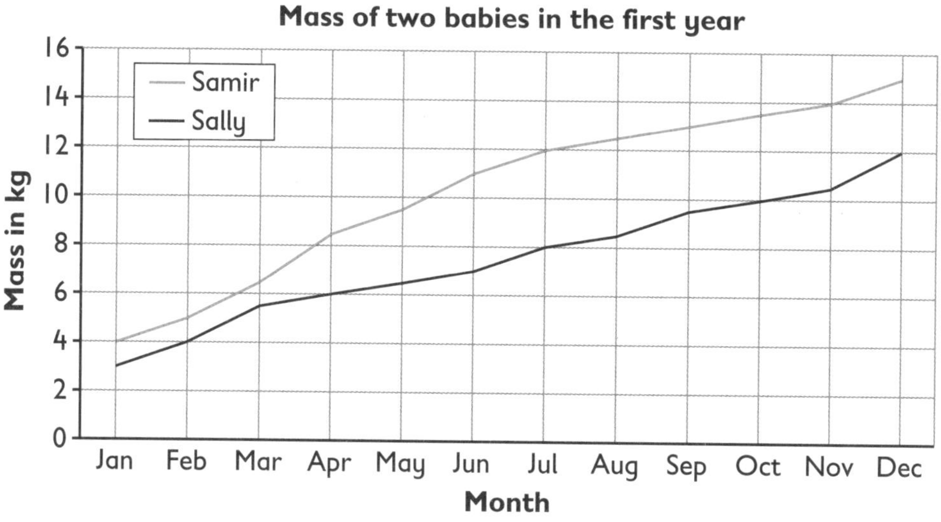

Mass of two babies in the first year

Legend: Samir, Sally

Y-axis: Mass in kg (0 to 16)
X-axis: Month (Jan, Feb, Mar, Apr, May, Jun, Jul, Aug, Sep, Oct, Nov, Dec)

Challenge 1

PS 1. What was Sally's mass in July?

1 mark

PS 2. What was Samir's mass in July?

1 mark

PS 3. How much heavier was Samir in July than Sally?

1 mark

PS 4. In which month did Sally reach a mass of 5 kg? _____

1 mark

Challenge 2

PS 1. How much heavier was Samir on 1st December than Sally?

1 mark

PS 2. Estimate the mass of Sally on 1st June.

1 mark

PS 3. How much heavier was Samir in July than in January?

1 mark

PS 4. Estimate the date and the month Samir's mass reached 13 kg. _____

1 mark

Challenge 3

PS 1. Samir's mass on 1st July was 12 kg.

How many months after that was it before Sally's mass was 12 kg?

1 mark

PS 2. For how many months did Sally have a mass of less than 8 kg?

1 mark

PS 3. Estimate the difference in the mass of Samir and Sally on 1st May.

1 mark

PS 4. Sally's mass on the 1st April was 6 kg.
Estimate the time it took for Sally's mass to increase another 3 kg.

1 mark

Total: ☐ / 12 marks

Had a go ☐   **Getting there** ☐   **Got it!** ☐

Progress test 6

1. a) 5,289 – 390 = _____   b) 5,339 + 2,678 = _____   c) 7,024 – 2,807 = _____

2. a) Tick the regular shape.

    b) Tick the irregular shape.

3. Convert these units.

    a) 4,000 g = _____ kg   b) 3.5 litres = _____ ml   c) 1,250 cm = _____ m

4. a) Find the area of this rectangle.   b) Find the area of this square.

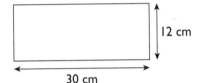

12 cm

30 cm _____

12 cm _____

5. Kendra fills a bucket that holds 12 litres of water. She uses it to fill a bird bath in her garden that holds 750 ml.

    How much water is left in the bucket?

    _____

6. Name these 3-D shapes.

    a) 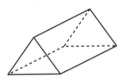   b)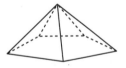

    _____   _____

7. Circle the number that has a digit with the value of forty thousand.

    64,920   154,817   460,192   7,424   148,357

8. $3^2 + 2^3 =$ ☐

9. Larry buys $3\frac{1}{4}$ kg of potatoes. When he puts them onto a set of digital scales that measures in kilograms, the reading is given as a decimal.

    What is the decimal reading?

    _____

PS 10. **This is a plan of Dev's garden. The garden is a rectangle. It has an area of 1,000 m².**

House	Garden

The house and garden are 20 metres wide.

How long is the garden? _____

1 mark

11. **Tick the angle that is a reflex angle.**

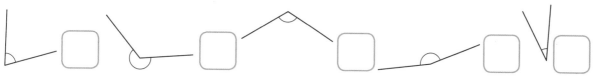

1 mark

12. a)   4,522 ÷ 34 = _____

b)   3,826 × 27 = _____

2 marks

PS 13. **At a concert, there are 6,388 seats. 5,176 tickets were sold on the Internet and 894 tickets were sold at the concert hall.**

How many tickets are left for sale? _____

1 mark

PS 14. **Five friends have the same homework for the weekend. They all do some of it on Friday.**

Harry does $\frac{1}{3}$ Kelly does $\frac{1}{6}$ Leo does $\frac{5}{12}$ Liz does $\frac{7}{24}$ May does $\frac{19}{48}$

Which friend has done most of their homework on Friday?

_____

1 mark

15. **Round 39.739 to:**

a)   the nearest whole number   _____   b)   the first decimal place   _____

2 marks

16. **Calculate the missing angles.**

a)

b)

2 marks

PS 17. **This table shows the types of fruit that are sold in a school shop one week.**

	Monday	Tuesday	Wednesday	Thursday	Friday	Total
Apples	25		22	24	28	131
Bananas				25	27	169
Pears	12	18	11	9	12	
Total	73	95	69	58	67	362

a)   How many pears were sold during the week?

b)   How many bananas were sold on Wednesday?

c)   How many bananas were sold on Tuesday?

3 marks

18. Draw the reflection of the shaded shape.

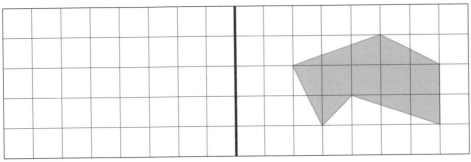

Mirror line

1 mark

PS 19. This is a train timetable.

Exeter	09:12	10:15	11:15	12:15	13:15
Tiverton	09:26	10:29	11:30	12:30	13:30
Taunton	09:39	10:42	11:43	12:43	13:43
Reading	11:09	12:04	13:12	14:04	15:12
London	11:34	12:29	13:35	14:27	15:37

a)   Poppy arrives at Exeter Station at 10 minutes to 11. She is travelling to Reading.

How long will it be before she arrives in Reading? _____

b)   Toni is leaving from Exeter and must be in Taunton for a meeting at half past 1.

It takes half an hour to reach the meeting place from Taunton Station.

Which is the latest train she can catch from Exeter? _____

c)   Which train from Exeter takes the shortest time to reach London?

_____

3 marks

20. Write these decimals in order, starting with the largest.

16.934   15.9   16.08   15.831   16.94

_____   _____   _____   _____   _____

1 mark

21. Find the perimeter of this hexagon.

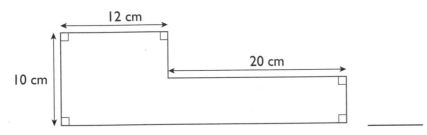

12 cm

20 cm

10 cm

_____

1 mark

22. Angle A and Angle B are equal. Find Angle B.

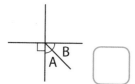

23. a) Translate the shaded square 5 squares left and 2 squares down.

  b) Translate the shaded triangle 6 squares right and 2 squares up.

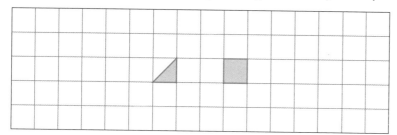

2 marks

24. Find Angle A in this rectangle.

1 mark

PS 25. This line graph shows rainfall in London. One line shows the average rainfall for each month in 2019 and the other line shows the average monthly rainfall between 1998 and 2018.

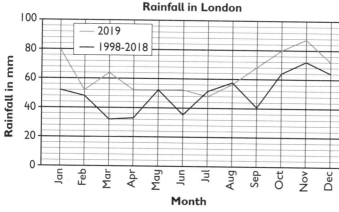

a) Which two months were driest overall between 1998 and 2018?

_____

b) Which month was wettest in 2019? _____

c) Estimate the average rainfall in November 2019. _____

d) Estimate how much wetter September was on average in 2019 compared with the previous 20 years.

_____

4 marks

Total: ☐ /43 marks

English mixed questions

1. **a)** Circle the facts and underline the opinions in the text below.

> Everybody wanted to watch this football match. There were 19,202 people in the stadium. During the game, James Trent scored 2 goals. He will soon be the best player in the country. United are now top of the league. Everyone will be happy with that.

6 marks

b) Choose one fact and explain what identifies it as a fact.

_____

c) Choose one opinion and explain what identifies it as opinion.

_____

2 marks

2. Label the words 1-6 to show the order in which they would appear in a dictionary.

belief   believe   believer   believable   believing   belie

1 mark

3. **Read the poem below.**

> **Wish**
> Holding tight,
> Wanting to forget,
> Holding back silent tears,
> Waiting for the pain to disappear,
> Holding,
> Holding,
> Holding,
> Wishing things could change.

a) Explain what sort of voice you think this poem should be read with.

_____

b) What do you think 'holding' refers to in this poem?

_____

_____

c) Why do you think the word 'holding' is used as the only word in three consecutive lines?

_____

_____

d) Why do you think this poem is called 'Wish'?

_____

_____

4 marks

4. **Rewrite each sentence, using a comma to remove any ambiguity.**

a) "It's time to get chopping children," said Dad with an axe in his hand.

_____

_____

b) There was juggling a man on stilts and a clown at the circus entrance.

_____

_____

2 marks

5. **Proofread the text and circle each spelling and punctuation error, writing the corrections for each below.**

It was a long way to the villige, which they could see in the distanse. Before them was a deep vally and a even deeper river   How would they cross it. Until they got their, they did not now but they were prepared whith ropes. First, they needed to rest before the next part of the advencher.

10 marks

6. **Look at the underlined words. Write the correct homophone.**

a)   She **aloud** her friend to borrow her computer.   _____

b)   The **advise** they were given was very useful.   _____

c)   I **guest** the answer but got it wrong.   _____

d)   The violin music will **proceed** the trumpet piece in the concert. _____

4 marks

7. **Use each given version of the word please (with its prefix and/or suffix) in a sentence.**

a)   pleasing

_____

_____

b)   pleasure

_____

_____

c)   displeased

_____

_____

d)   unpleasurable

_____

_____

4 marks

8. **Write the root word for each pair of words.**

a)   attending, attendance   _____

b)   hearing, misheard   _____

c)   equality, unequal   _____

d)   reliable, unreliable   _____

4 marks

9. **Underline the silent letter in each word then write a sentence containing that word.**

a)   column

_____

_____

b) receipt

_____

_____

c) muscle

_____

_____

d) scene

_____

_____

e) wreck

_____

_____

5 marks

10. **Write each piece of information in the correct column of the table to show whether it belongs in paragraph 1 or paragraph 2.**

a blue and red racing car   a large number 7 on the roof

fast and furious as the cars sped along   the fastest car

a powerful engine   the growl of several engines

a crash and pile up   the crowd cheered

Paragraph 1: The car	Paragraph 2: The race

8 marks

11. **Circle the correct relative pronoun to use in each sentence.**

a) They went to the shop **which / where** they had seen the dress for sale.

b) The car **that / who** his mum drives is really cool.

c) We ate Em's chocolate cake, **who / which** was very tasty.

d) The city **that / where** they were born is very busy.

4 marks

12. **Write a dictionary definition for each word below. Give the word class(es) for each word.**

father _____

_____

farther _____

_____

descent _____

_____

decent _____

_____

steal _____

_____

steel _____

_____

13. **Underline the adverb in each sentence.**

    a) The small boat drifted peacefully across the serene blue lake.

    b) Zac stomped his bare feet angrily on the stairs and shouted to his dad.

    c) She visited her horses at the stables in the village daily.

    d) They decided to sail nearby, on the large river that flowed through town.

4 marks

14. **Tick the sentences that use parentheses correctly.**

    a) My cousins all live in Watford (a town near) London.

    b) The flight, despite a 20-minute delay in taking off, arrived on time.

    c) Their dog – a funny, friendly – and old poodle was very cute.

    d) The snow (which had not been forecast) started at 10pm.

    e) Nobody, not even the teachers could, work out the answer.

1 mark

15. **Write the correct form of the verb to complete each sentence.**

    a) Amy _____ a cake last Sunday. (**bake**)

    b) Yannick went _____ when he got to the hotel. (**swim**)

    c) When we arrive, I shall _____ a meal. (**cook**)

    d) Nobody _____ what the magician did. (**see**)

4 marks

16. **Read the text below.**

    The performers received a standing ovation. It was hardly surprising as this had
    been such a wonderful musical. The costumes, dancing, and of course the acting, were
    amazing but the music and singing were a shining light.

    The stunts too were incredible. The danger was clear to see with action at great heights
    and nerve-wracking balancing, all taking place among the intricate scenery created on and
    above the stage.

a)   Name four aspects of the musical praised in the text.

_____   _____

_____   _____

b)   Find and copy the metaphor used in the text.

_____

_____

c)   What two things does the text suggest were dangerous about the stunts?

_____

_____

d)   Explain why the text has been split into two paragraphs.

_____

_____

8 marks

17. a)   Write a sentence about a person you know that is fact.

_____

_____

b)   Write a sentence about a person you know that is opinion.

_____

_____

2 marks

18. **Write a summary of a story you know, using three sentences.**

_____

_____

_____

_____

_____

_____

3 marks

19. **Read the text below.**

Moonlight danced on the gently swaying surface of the sea. All was calm and the only sound was the oars dipping into the water and the gentle snoring of her dog, Max, curled up on the floor beneath her feet. She felt relaxed even after rowing for several hours, and she knew she could row for several more. She took in the beauty of the water beneath her, the bay around her and the stars like diamonds shining in their millions in the clear sky.

But in that water beneath her, something stirred. The creature was having no luck in its search for fish but right now it did not care. It had noticed the small rowing boat pass above. It knew the boat and its occupants would be no match for the strength of its jaws.

a)   What simile is used in the text?

_____

b) What does the text tell us about the character's rowing ability?

_____

_____

c) Why is the text split into two paragraphs?

_____

_____

_____

d) What do you predict will happen next? Explain your prediction.

_____

_____

_____

4 marks

20. Circle the correct homophone or near-homophone in each sentence.

a) The children were very **wary / weary** after travelling all day.

b) They were asked to show the **guessed / guest** around school.

c) On the motorway they **passed / past** a huge truck carrying a boat.

d) We had a lovely **desert / dessert** at the restaurant.

4 marks

21. Read the extract and then answer the questions.

> The zoo was very busy and Mum had to keep calling to Freddie as he kept trying to run ahead. I held on to Mum's hand as I was frightened of losing her.
>
> "The lions are just up ahead," called Freddie excitedly. "Hurry up you two!"
>
> Mum quickened her pace to try to catch up with Freddie, pulling me along with her by the hand.
>
> Moments later, we turned the corner to the lion enclosure and were faced with a huge, majestic lion right behind the bars of the cage. I gasped. He was so big! I hid behind Mum.
>
> "Look, Sophie, look!" cried Freddie. "Isn't he amazing?" Freddie gazed in awe at the great creature as it stood there like a proud statue.
>
> Later that day, the zoo seemed to have got even busier. I felt completely swamped by people. Suddenly, Mum gripped my hand more tightly and started to run.
>
> "Freddie!" she was shouting, "Freddie!"

a) Give two examples of adverbials of time from the extract.

_____

_____

b) Find and copy a simile from the text.

_____

_____

c) Give two examples of adverbs from the text.

_____

d) What tense is the extract written in?

_____

e) What do you infer about how the main character feels about seeing the lion? Give evidence from the text to support your answer.

_____

_____

_____

f) What do you predict might happen next?

_____

_____

6 marks

22. These sentences are missing a word containing a silent letter. Write the missing silent letter word to complete each sentence.

a) A human hand has four fingers and a _____.

b) I walked up the path at the front of the house and _____ on the door.

c) I was so cold, my fingers had gone _____.

d) I need a pair of _____ to cut the paper.

e) The bath was leaking so my mum phoned a _____ to come and fix it.

f) On Hallowe'en, my sister put a white sheet over her head and said she was dressing up as a _____.

6 marks

23. a) Write two facts about yourself.

_____

_____

_____

_____

b) Write two opinions about your home, family or pet.

_____

_____

_____

_____

4 marks

Total: [   ] / 106 marks

Maths mixed questions

1. Find the missing numbers in these number sequences.

   a) 10,730   11,730   _____   13,730   14,730

   b) 132,080   _____   _____   129,080   128,080

   c) 260,600   _____   _____   _____   220,600

    3 marks

2. a) 56 + 55 = _____

   b) 2,680 + 200 = _____

   c) 547 − 98 = _____

    3 marks

PS 3. Javid has a collection of 326 football cards. 138 are in colour.
   The rest are black and white.

   How many of the football cards are in black and white? _____

   1 mark

4. Write these fractions as decimals.

   a) $\frac{4}{10}$ = _____

   b) $\frac{73}{100}$ = _____

   c) $\frac{7}{100}$ = _____

   d) $\frac{6}{1,000}$ = _____

   e) $\frac{203}{1,000}$ = _____

    5 marks

PS 5. Nia checks her purse. She has two £20 notes, three £5 notes and £6.73 in coins.

   She spends £28.55 on some shopping.

   How much money does she have left? _____

    1 mark

PS 6. As part of a school project, Charlie records the temperature each Saturday at midday for 6 weeks. He records the results as a line graph.

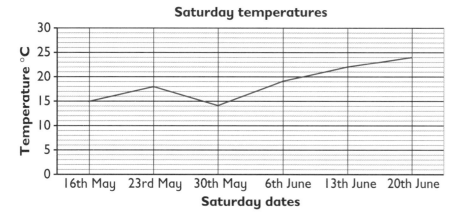

   Saturday temperatures

   a) What temperature did Charlie record on 30th May?   _____

   b) On how many Saturdays was the temperature below 20 °C?   _____

   c) How much warmer was 20th June than 30th May?   _____

   3 marks

7. Circle the numbers that are factors of 60.

   3   4   8   12   15   20

   1 mark

PS 8. **This table shows the population of five UK cities.**

City	Coventry	Manchester	Preston	Stoke	Sunderland
Population	359,262	395,515	313,332	372,775	335,415

Write the cities in order of the size of their population, starting with the largest.

_____ _____ _____ _____ _____

1 mark

9. **Work out the following:**

a) $\frac{3}{4} - \frac{5}{12} =$ _____

b) $\frac{7}{15} + \frac{2}{3} =$ _____

c) $\frac{4}{5} - \frac{3}{20} =$ _____

3 marks

10. **Complete this table with the missing measurements of these rectangles.**

	Length	Width	Perimeter	Area
a)	12 cm	8 cm		
b)	30 cm	20 cm		
c)		7 cm	32 cm	
d)			20 cm	25 cm²

8 marks

11. **Draw a reflection of the shape.**

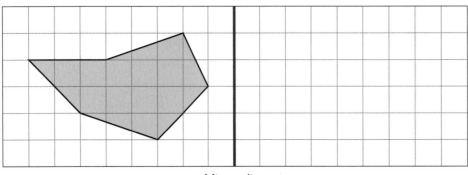

Mirror line

1 mark

PS 12. **Manisha cuts a pizza into 12 equal pieces. She puts 6 of the pieces onto a plate.**

Manisha says, "I have put $\frac{6}{12}$ of the pizza onto the plate."

Her mother says, "No, you have put $\frac{1}{2}$ of the pizza onto the plate."

Explain who is correct.

_____

_____

1 mark

PS 13. **Jay completes a maths test of 60 one-mark questions.**

When he gets his paper back, the teacher has written 80% on the paper.

How many questions did Jay get correct?

1 mark

PS 14. **A local building has these Roman numerals written above the door to show the year it was opened:**

MCMXII

In what year was the building opened? _____

1 mark

15. a)   6,291 − 2,278 = _____

b)   4,628 + 2,684 = _____

2 marks

16. **Circle the shape that is always a regular shape.**

    triangle   square   pentagon   hexagon   octagon

1 mark

PS 17. **Noah finds an old recipe book. The recipe asks for $\frac{1}{2}$ pound of flour.**

He knows 450 g is approximately I pound.
He has a full 2-kilogram bag of flour.

Approximately how much flour is left in the bag in grams if he takes $\frac{1}{2}$ pound out?

_____

1 mark

PS 18. **This table shows information about the population of a town.**

Age	0–11 years	12–17 years	18–64 years	65 years and over
Male	3,446	2,837	26,531	3,289
Female	3,278	2,688	25,749	4,653

a)   How many males are aged 64 years or less?   _____

b)   How many people are aged 17 or less?   _____

c)   How many more male than female 18–64 year olds are there?   _____

3 marks

PS 19. **It takes 101 hours to sail from the eastern end of the Mediterranean Sea to the western end.**

How long is this in days and hours?   _____

1 mark

20. **Calculate:**

a) 12^2 = _____

b) 10^3 = _____

c) $5^3 − 5^2$ = _____

3 marks

PS 21. **Maisie weighs some sugar on a set of digital scales. The scales read 0.528 kg.**

She rounds the amount to one decimal place.

To what amount does Maisie round the number?   _____

1 mark

22. **Complete this table to show fraction, decimal and percentage equivalents.**

Fraction		Decimal		Percentage
$\frac{3}{4}$	=		=	
	=		=	80%
	=	0.95	=	

6 marks

137

23. Circle the value of the digit 7 in the number 897,425.

seven hundred   seven hundred thousand   seventy

   seventy thousand   seven thousand

1 mark

PS 24. This drawing shows Rose's fish tank.
   The fish tank is 60 cm long, 20 cm wide and 30 cm high.
   The water fills the tank to 5 cm from the top.

   How much water is in the tank in litres? _____

1 mark

25. Tick all the obtuse angles.

1 mark

26. Round 109,046

   a) to the nearest 100 _____

   b) the nearest 100,000 _____

   c) to the nearest 10,000 _____

   d) the nearest 10 _____

4 marks

27. Calculate and then write the inverse calculation to check your answer for:

   a) $9,043 - 2,091 =$ _____

   b) $82,714 + 4,827 =$ _____

2 marks

28. List all the prime numbers between 50 and 60 _____

1 mark

PS 29. Tara, Beth, Jan and Nisha share some money. Tara takes $\frac{1}{5}$ of the money, Beth takes $\frac{3}{10}$, Jan takes $\frac{5}{20}$ and Nisha takes $\frac{1}{4}$

   Who takes the most money? _____

1 mark

PS 30. A farmer measures the length of one of his fields.

   He says that the field is 100 yards long and 80 yards wide.

   Approximately how long and wide are these measurements in metres?

   length = _____   width = _____

2 marks

31. **Write these decimals in order, smallest first.**

a) 7.903   7.93   7.039   7.093

_____ _____ _____ _____

b) 17.865   16.965   16.695   17.86

_____ _____ _____ _____

2 marks

PS 32. **Pippa says, "This is a regular decagon because it has ten sides and all the sides are the same length."**

Explain why Pippa is incorrect.

_____

_____

1 mark

PS 33. **This graph shows temperatures inside and outside for one day.**

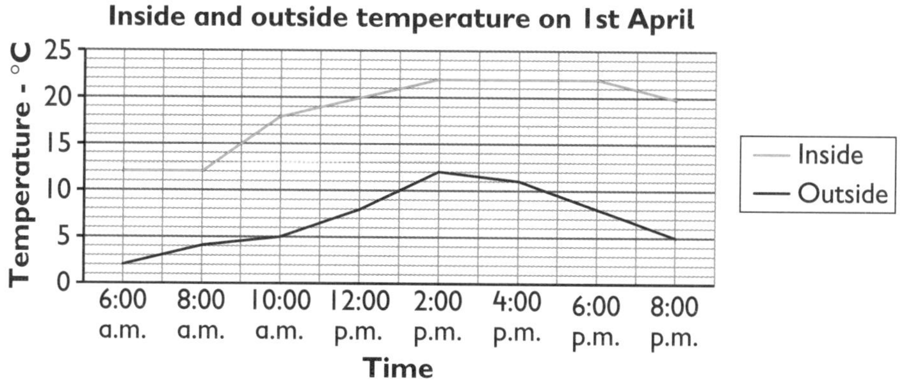

Inside and outside temperature on 1st April

a) What was the outside temperature at 10:00 a.m.?

_____

b) What was the difference in the outside temperature at 6:00 a.m. and 6:00 p.m.?

_____

c) For how long was the outside temperature above 10 °C?

_____

d) What was the difference between the inside and outside temperatures at 5:00 p.m.?

_____

4 marks

34. **These angles are on straight angles. Find the missing angles.**

a)

141°
?

b)

78°   ?

These angles all show a full turn. Find the missing angles.

c)

321°
?

d)

158°
?

4 marks

PS 35. **The temperature inside a classroom is 21 °C.**
Outside the temperature is –2 °C.

What is the difference between the two temperatures? _____

1 mark

PS 36. **This is a timetable for trains from York.**

York	09:45	10:18	10:51	11:18	11:45	12:18
Northallerton		10:31		11:31		12:31
Darlington	10:16	10:48	11:22	11:50	12:17	12:49
Durham	10:33	11:04		12:05		13:03
Newcastle	10:45	11:16	11:54	12:17	12:43	13:15

a) Matt arrives at Darlington Station at five minutes to 11 and catches the next train to Newcastle.

At what time will he arrive in Newcastle? _____

b) Josie wants to catch a train from York. She must be in Newcastle before half past twelve.

Which would be the latest train she could catch from York? _____

c) Dev wants to catch a train from Darlington to Durham. He arrives at Darlington Station at quarter past eleven.

How long will he have to wait for the next train to Durham? _____

d) A train from Northallerton to York takes as long as the 12:18 train from York to Northallerton.

If the train from Northallerton leaves at 14:05, when will it arrive in York?

_____

4 marks

PS 37. **Mo draws a point on a coordinate grid at the coordinates (7, 12).**

He translates the point 7 squares left and 5 squares up.

What are the new coordinates for Mo's point? _____

1 mark

38. **Draw the shape in the translated positions.**

   a) 8 squares right, 1 square up

   b) 4 squares left, 2 squares down

   c) 2 squares right, 2 squares down

   d) 6 squares left, 1 square up

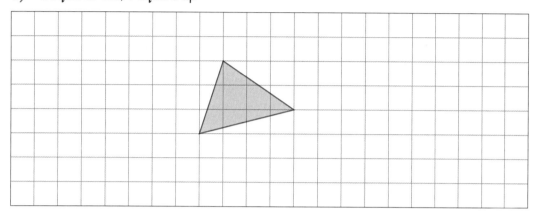

4 marks

39. a) 4.8 × _____ = 480

   b) 506 ÷ _____ = 5.06

   c) 0.076 × _____ = 76

3 marks

PS 40. **Kate and Sid go walking. They use different maps.**

   Kate's map has a scale of 5 cm to 12 km and Sid's map has a scale of 1 cm to 8 km.
   Kate's route is 2.5 cm on the map and Sid's route is also 2.5 cm on his map.

   How much longer is Sid's route than Kate's route? _____

1 mark

41. **Find the missing number.**

   a) $\frac{3}{10} \times \boxed{} = \frac{9}{10}$

   b) $\frac{1}{12} \times \boxed{} = \frac{1}{2}$

   c) $\frac{2}{3} \times \boxed{} = 1\frac{1}{3}$

   d) $\frac{2}{5} \times \boxed{} = 1\frac{3}{5}$

   e) $\frac{3}{4} \times \boxed{} = 3\frac{3}{4}$

5 marks

42. **Change these fractions to decimals.**

   a) $\frac{7}{100} =$ _____

   b) $\frac{9}{1,000} =$ _____

   c) $\frac{509}{1,000} =$ _____

   d) $\frac{500}{10} =$ _____

   e) $\frac{209}{100} =$ _____

   f) $\frac{7,345}{1,000} =$ _____

6 marks

PS 43. Jack is going to buy a new car so he checks the widths of the cars in a car magazine to see if they will fit in his garage.

The car widths are:

1.645 m   1.708 m   1.784 m   1.63 m   1.71 m

a)   Write the car widths in order, starting with the narrowest.

_____   _____   _____   _____   _____

b)   How many of the cars are wider than $1\frac{3}{4}$ metres?

c)   How many of the cars are narrower than 170 centimetres?

3 marks

PS 44. Donny is travelling by train from his home to go to see his grandma.

It takes him 20 minutes to get from his house to the station and then he has to wait a quarter of an hour for the train. The train journey is $2\frac{3}{4}$ hours and then it takes him 25 minutes to walk to his grandma's house.

How long does it take Donny to get from his house to his grandma's house?

_____

1 mark

PS 45. Complete the table of measurements of rectangles to show the lengths of the missing sides.

	Length	Width	Perimeter	Area
a)	12 cm		48 cm	
b)		9 cm		90 cm²
c)	20 cm		60 cm	
d)		6 cm		120 cm²
e)	25 cm		62 cm	

10 marks

46. Reflect the shape in the mirror line.

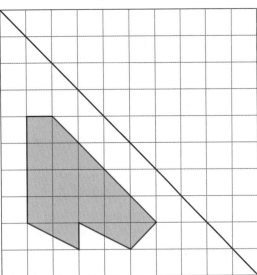

1 mark

142

(PS) **47. Find the missing numbers.**

a)
```
    6 8 □ 4
  -   □ 2 5 9
  ---------
    5 5 5 5
```

b)
```
    7 3 □ 5
  + □ 8 8 3
  ---------
    9 2 3 8
```

c)
```
        4 3 5
    ×     □ 6
    ---------
      2 6 1 0
    □ 7 0 0
    ---------
    1 1 3 1 0
```

d)
```
        8 0 □
    ×     □ 7
    ---------
      5 6 2 1
    4 0 1 5 0
    ---------
    4 5 7 7 1
```

4 marks

(PS) **48. A school is hoping to raise £500 for charity. The table shows how much has been raised.**

Class	1S	2F	3B	4R	5D	6K
Money raised	£65.27	£57.76	£49.54	£84.80	£67.35	£78.42

How much more is needed to reach the target of £500?

_____

1 mark

49. 12 – 15 – 8 = □

 1 mark

50. These angles are right angles. Find the missing angles.

a)

68° ? □

b) 11°

? □

2 marks

51. The temperature during the day is 7°C. The temperature falls by 10°C at night.

What is the temperature at night? □

1 mark

52. Write any common multiple of 3 and 8 □

1 mark

53. Find the missing numerator.

$$\frac{2}{12} + \frac{\square}{12} = \frac{9}{12}$$

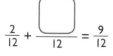
1 mark

Total: □ / 126 marks

Answers

ENGLISH

Page 5

Challenge 1

1. **a)** act **b)** like **c)** employ **d)** house **e)** read **f)** visit

Challenge 2

1. explain, curious, add, suffice, recognise

Challenge 3

1. Accept any word which makes sense and uses the given suffix or prefix. Examples: **a)** slowly **b)** brightly **c)** unkind **d)** hopeful **e)** impossible **f)** rediscover

2. **a)** helpful　　**b)** argument　　**c)** destruction

3. **a)** adjective　　**b)** noun　　**c)** noun

Page 7

Challenge 1

1. **a)** <u>mis</u> **b)** <u>un</u> **c)** <u>ment</u> **d)** <u>able</u> **e)** <u>est</u> **f)** <u>il</u> **g)** <u>im</u> **h)** <u>ous</u>

Challenge 2

1. **a)** explained **b)** explanation **c)** unexplained **d)** explaining **e)** explain **f)** explains

Challenge 3

1. **a)** unkind **b)** misunderstand **c)** helpfully **d)** unreliable **e)** disqualified **f)** divisible **g)** unimpressed **h)** incomplete

2. **a)** noun **b)** noun **c)** adjective **d)** adverb **e)** adjective

Page 9

Challenge 1

1. **a)** love story **C** **b)** betrayal **A** **c)** friendship **B** **d)** adventure **B** **e)** crime **A** **f)** magic **C**

Challenge 2

1. Examples: **a)** … her broken heart needs mending… ; He does all he can to help and falls in love with her.
   b) … jealous friend trying to frame her.
   c) … they learn to like and trust each other
   d) … they spend many days and nights crossing jungles, mountains and rivers
   e) … needs to find out who is making money disappear; she makes a new discovery she also gets closer to danger
   f) … tells him how a spell changed her

Challenge 3

1. **a)** An accurate assessment of the theme of the chosen article.
   b) Identification of conventions in the article, e.g. explaining, persuading.

2. **a)** An accurate assessment of the theme of the chosen book.
   b) Identification of conventions in characters and plot for the chosen book.

Page 11

Challenge 1

1. meow – cat; sizzle – sausages; tweet – bird; ding – bell; pop – balloons

Challenge 2

1. **a)** The clouds were – like balls of cotton wall.
   b) The large man was – as tall as a tree.
   c) Nina ran – as fast as a train.
   d) Her temper was – as vicious as a tiger.

2. Various choices are possible. Examples:
   a) **The sun** was a burning disc in the blue sky.
   b) The moonlight was **a torch lighting the way**.
   c) The snow was **white feathers drifting slowly to Earth**.

Challenge 3

1. **a)** boom (of distant thunder)
   b) removing the grass like lawnmowers
   c) the rain that followed was a wave…
   d) Giraffes stood splendidly statuesque

Page 13

Challenge 1

1. Each word must fit with the context of the characters' speech. Examples: **a)** boldly, bravely, confidently
   b) meanly, menacingly, threateningly
   c) mocking, taunting, boastfully
   d) threateningly, meanly, menacingly, confidently

2. Examples: **a)** Knight: brave, strong and self-assured
   b) Dragon: evil, old and dangerous

Challenge 2

1. **a)** Then the banging, breaking, smashing, shattering.
   b) Any suitable reason. Examples: It towers over its surroundings./It is so tall./It is tall and made of concrete, which might make it look like a monster./It is made of concrete, which is strong and hard.

Challenge 3

1. The answer given should refer to the noise of demolition (indicating a change of tone in the poem) and/or the destruction that these words suggest.

2. The given answer should be justified with reference to the poem. Example: Sadly because it's like the monster is now destroyed (rubble), or quietly because there is now just rubble and a silent cloud of dust.

Page 15

Challenge 1

1. **a)** O **b)** F **c)** F **d)** O **e)** O **f)** F

Challenge 2

1. **Facts:** The English Channel is 34km wide at its narrowest point.
   People attempt to swim this each year.
   There are hazards such as ships to avoid.
   To complete the channel swim you need to be a strong swimmer.
   Opinions: It is a really silly thing to do.
   Swimmers need to be brave.
   All swimmers enjoy the experience.
   It is much better to stick to going for walks for your exercise.

2. The explanation should acknowledge that facts can be proved and opinions can differ from one person to the next.

Challenge 3

1. Each answer must clearly be fact or opinion as indicated. Examples: **a)** My house has 3 bedrooms. (fact)
   b) My house is the best on the street. (opinion)
   c) I like swimming, which is a good form of exercise. (fact)
   d) Collecting coins is the best hobby. (opinion)

Page 17

Challenge 1

1. dangerous
2. a)–c) Cars drive too quickly; There are no safe places to cross; There is no proper place to park to drop-off and pick-up children.

Challenge 2

1. a) dozens
   b) Provide a safe place to cross. OR Lower the speed limit. OR Widen the footpath. OR Provide a safe place to park for drop-off and pick-up.

Challenge 3

1. Any four from: so dangerous; lower speed limit; cars drive far too quickly; a safe place to cross; proper place to park; footpath is narrow; dozens of near misses; somebody will get seriously injured, or worse; puts in place urgent safety measures; protect all pedestrians
2. The summary must include the main points that there is a dangerous road outside the school and that urgent safety measures are needed to protect people. Example: The road outside the school is dangerous and putting lives at risk. Parents are demanding urgent safety measures are put in place.

Page 19

Challenge 1

1. Any two from (or other reasonable predictions):
   - The thugs might catch/kidnap/hurt Carter.
   - The thugs are working for the Storkman.
   - Carter might hide/escape.
   - There might be a fight.
   - Somebody rescues Carter.

Challenge 2

1. Alice started to push each crayon down in the pencil pot.
2. Alice may have felt left out or she may have felt nervous/strange with new people.

Challenge 3

1. a) It probably had not been entered for a long time.
   b) He had a secret life. OR He had been involved in something adventurous/exciting/mysterious.
   c) Whoever is looking through the attic finds out what is in the brown leather folder/what the Top Secret is, leading to an adventure of some sort.

Pages 20–23

Progress test 1: English

1. a) talking b) looked c) misread d) approved e) unkind
2. The graceful dolphins dive deep into the ocean. ✓
   The wind whistled and wailed through the door. ✓
3. a) Her voice was booming – as loud as thunder.
   b) They were up and down – like a yo-yo.
   c) Sam crept along – as quietly as a mouse.
   d) The beach was – like a small desert.
4. a) disappearing b) invisible c) misunderstood
   d) impossible e) unfortunately
5. a) Example: bored, moaning
   b) Example: laughing, giggling, jokingly
   c) Example: seriously, whispering
6. a) Example: She is brave. She is determined.
   b) She was doing something difficult even though 'her hands and knees continued to bleed.' 'She wanted to cry but she knew she must go on.'

c) Example: She gets to the top of the mountain. She slips/falls. (Any reasonable answer.)
   d) Example: She is brave and determined and this means she will succeed. If she falls it will add tension to the story and make it more exciting.
7. Examples: a) misheard/misunderstood/misread
   b) kindly/carefully/respectfully c) disliked/disowned
   d) unwrapped e) careful f) helping g) impossible
   h) illegible
8. a) Two from: Last year I went on holiday (with my parents); I went… to Orlando.; Orlando is in Florida.; We went to watch a baseball game; The Tampa Bay Rays won the game.; I swam in the pool every day.
   b) Two from: … a baseball game, which was amazing.; The stadium had a fantastic atmosphere; The weather was perfect.; It was the best holiday ever.
9. a) excitable b) exciting c) excitement d) unexcited
10. Opinion because it may not be very pleasant and relaxing for everyone, and not all people may find the views from the windows interesting.
11. Examples:
    a) a sunny, sparkling smile
    b) the curious, cunning cat
    c) a horrible, haunted house
    d) the slow, sticky slug
12. a) Two from: fine sand like flour; wind whipping waves; frenzied foam
    b) fine sand like flour; people like quiet mice
    c) Wild rivers flowing into the drains.
    d) onomatopoeia
    e) The first seven lines might be read quickly (and maybe loudly too) to represent the wind, rain and noise of the storm. The final two lines could then be read quietly and calmly.
13. a) noun b) adverb c) adjective d) adjective e) noun
    f) noun

MATHS

Page 25

Challenge 1

1. a) 5,054   5,154
   b) 37,600   37,590
   c) 97,893   107,893
2. 50,702 circled
3. 5,820   5,802   5,280   5,208   5,028

Challenge 2

1. a) 19,927 b) 129,087 c) 779,952
2. a) 51,627 b) twenty thousand and forty-six
3. 34,502   34,025   32,450   32,405   32,045

Challenge 3

1. a) 792,261   782,261   …   762,261
   b) 368,288   369,288   370,288
   c) 96,452   97,452   …   99,452
2. 446,036 circled

Page 27

Challenge 1

1. a) 30 or thirty b) 40,000 or forty thousand c) 5,000 or five thousand
2. a) 39 b) 77 c) 109
3. a) 45,280 b) 45,000 c) 50,000

Challenge 2

1. 481,239   1,982,732   81,634   circled
2. CXLV   CCXX   XCVI   CDIX   XXII

    22   96   145   220   409

3. a) 804,800 b) 800,000 c) 800,000

Challenge 3

1. Any number with the digits shown: 557,5**
2. a) DCLX b) XXII   c) CLXX
3. 834,867 and 826,025 circled

Page 29

Challenge 1

1. a) 3 °C circled b) 0 °C circled c) –3 °C circled
2. a) –1 b) –3   c) –4
3. a) 3   b) 2   c) 7

Challenge 2

1. a) 2   b) –8
2. –3
3. a) 11 °C   b) 15 °C   c) 14 °C   d) 5 °C

Challenge 3

1. a) 25 °C   b) 13 °C
2. a) 18 °C b) Berlin c) Sydney and Moscow (both)
    d) 3 (Accept London, Sydney and Miami)

Page 31

Challenge 1

1. a) 78   b) 45   c) 151
2. a) 1,395   b) 484 c) 640
3. 406   406 + 429 = 835
4. a) 6,000   b) 15,000

Challenge 2

1. a) 653   b) 1,140   c) 696
2. a) 2,648   b) 89,323   c) 17,517
3. 4,056   4,056 + 4,719 = 8,775
4. a) 50,000 b) 110,000

Challenge 3

1. a) 61,000 b) 69,100   c) 110,300
2. a) 232,498 b) 702,532 c) 702,680
3. a) 300,803   300,803 + 7,312 = 308,115
    b) 251,790   251,790 – 242,456 = 9,334
4. a) 700,000 b) 600,000

Page 33

Challenge 1

1. 18
2. (1, 24), (2, 12), (3, 8), (4, 6)
3. 2, 11 and 17 circled   4. 2 and 11
5. a) 25 b) 8   c) 100

Challenge 2

1. 63, 84 and 105 circled
2. (1, 36), (2, 18), (3, 12), (4, 9), (6, 6)
3. 3   4. 315
5. a) 8   b) 4   c) 12

Challenge 3

1. a) 12 b) 24   c) 18
2. a) 4   b) 8   c) 9
3. (1, 48), (2, 24), (3, 16), (4, 12), (6, 8)
4. 83   89
5. a) 36 and 64   b) 25 and 16

Page 35

Challenge 1

1. a) 210 b) 800
2. a) 128   b) 130   c) 17
3. a) 5,700 b) 49.3   c) 3,760   d) 69.8   e) 7.12

Challenge 2

1. a) 630 b) 40
2. a) 228 b) 340   c) 264 d) 25   e) 30
3. a) 0.83 b) 5.08   c) 89   d) 1,000   e) 30.06

Challenge 3

1. a) 6   b) 8   c) 8,100
2. a) 16,800 b) 1,400   c) 3,042 d) 5   e) 1,200
3. a) 100   b) 1,000   c) 1,000 d) 100   e) 100

Page 37

Challenge 1

1. a) 3,368   b) 1,422   c) 3,125   d) 1,992   e) 4,256
2. a) 1,152   b) 2,080   c) 896   d) 2,268   e) 5,712
3. a) 248   b) 105   c) 83   d) 82   e) 56

Challenge 2

1. a) 9,580   b) 13,035   c) 27,162 d) 36,496 e) 25,524
2. a) 20,072 b) 17,325   c) 33,712 d) 45,657 e) 41,664
3. a) 1,711   b) 1,405   c) 768   d) 633   e) 686

Challenge 3

1. a) 39,402   b) 30,032   c) 49,203 d) 1,248 e) 984
2. a) 430,400 b) 168,275 c) 349,104 d) 54
3. a) 2,460   b) 1,288   c) 622   d) 3,105 e) 997

Page 39

Challenge 1

1. 864 (tins)   2. 1,648 (tickets)   3. 12,208
4. 9 (years old)

Challenge 2

1. 5,236 (seats)   2. 75 (bags)
3. Possible answers:
    2 books have 4 stars and 9 books have 5 stars
    7 books have 4 stars and 5 books have 5 stars
    12 books have 4 stars and 1 book has 5 stars
4. 2 (minutes)

Challenge 3

1. 49,170 (passengers)
2. 304 (filled boxes)
3. Possible answers:
    £20 × 3, £10 × 1, £5 × 1
    £20 × 2, £10 × 3, £5 × 1
    £20 × 2, £10 × 2, £5 × 3
    £20 × 2, £10 × 1, £5 × 5
    £20 × 1, £10 × 5, £5 × 1
    £20 × 1, £10 × 4, £5 × 3
    £20 × 1, £10 × 3, £5 × 5
    £20 × 1, £10 × 2, £5 × 7
    £20 × 1, £10 × 1, £5 × 9
4. 10 (km)

Pages 40–43

Progress test 2: maths

1. a) 29,830   b) 709,882
2. a) 265,024 circled   b) 378,209 circled
3. a) 8,212   b) 5,091
4. a) 49   b) 64
5. a) 676 b) 788   c) 218   d) 674
6. 34,675   34,756   34,765   35,476   35,674

7. 6,767 (spectators)   8. 13,000
9. (1, 48), (2, 24), (3, 16), (4, 12), (6, 8)
10. a) 3,000   b) 60,000   c) 183,000   d) 910,000
11. −5 (°C)
12. a) 39   b) 79   c) 94   d) 48
13. a) 4,302   b) 2,595   c) 9,511
14. a) 50,067   b) 204,506 c) 920,078
15. 36,769
16. a) 2,800   b) 378   c) 13
17. 31   37   18. 6,825 (peacocks)   19. 2014
20. 782 × 7 = 5,474
21. 281 (bracelets)
22. a) 41,610   b) 1,118   c) 570   d) 72,424   e) 1,334
23. (Floor) 5
24. a) 500,000   b) 528,900   c) 529,000
25. a) 6,389 + 2,584 = 8,973   b) 7,083 − 2,479 = 4,604
26. 6,262 (comics)
27. Dalfield (Accept 103,092)
28. a) 12   b) 12
29. 9,423   30. 7 (°C)   31. 87,000
32. a) 35,099 b) 24,995 c) 5,000
33. 2,500 (boxes)   34. 28,200 (fans)
35. a) −4   b) −11   c) −1
36. 6,250 (points)
37. a) 6,578 × 4 = 26,312   b) 5,274 ÷ 6 = 879
38. 1,344
39. length = 6 m and width = 3.6 m
40. a) 10 b) 100

ENGLISH
Page 45
Challenge 1
1. im − practical; in − sane; un − usual; re − appear; il − legal
2. Examples: a) unfortunate b) illegible c) impossible
    d) incompetent e) reaction
Challenge 2
1. a) **un**popular b) **re**arrange c) **dis**regard
    d) **mis**understanding
2. Examples: a) reset b) illegible c) immature
Challenge 3
1. Each sentence should use the word correctly.
    Examples:
    a) They were **unheard** of outside of their home town.
    b) She had to **reheat** the food.
    c) Nobody should **mistreat** a pet.
    d) He had to **rearrange** the meeting.

Page 47
Challenge 1
1. a) length**en**, final**ise**, solid**ify**, b) test**ify**, valid**ate**,
    visual**ise**, c) special**ise**, soft**en**, advert**ise** d) tight**en**,
    elastic**ate**, hard**en**
Challenge 2
1. a) The final letter is doubled before adding -en.
    b) The **y** is dropped before adding -ise.
    c) The **or** ending is dropped before adding -ify.
2. Examples:
    a) The farmer had to **fatten** the animals before taking
       them to market.
    b) Everybody could **sympathise** with her point of view.
    c) If she let the spider out, she knew it would **terrify**
       her brother.

Challenge 3
1. a) The e is dropped before adding the suffix: fortune
    → fortunate; pure → purify. b) Examples: They were
    fortunate to have no homework.; They had to purify
    the water before drinking it.

Page 49
Challenge 1
1. a) space b) infect c) office d) part e) race
Challenge 2
1. a) cautious b) essential c) fictitious d) confidential
2. a) delicious b) official c) essential d) contentious
Challenge 3
1. a) suspicious b) nutritious c) malicious d) commercial
2. a) palace – palatial
       This is tricky because the c in palace changes to a t
       in palatial.
    b) fierce – ferocious
       This is tricky because the root word changes beyond
       recognition.

Page 51
Challenge 1
1. b, g, k, w
2. a) m b) n c) n d) r or h
Challenge 2
1. a) lam**b** b) **w**ren c) colum**n** d) s**c**ene e) **w**hole f) si**g**n
2. a) gnat – a very small flying insect
    b) gnash – to grind the teeth
Challenge 3
1. a) Example: ca**l**m The sea was very calm.
    b) Example: hym**n** They joined in with the hymn.
    c) Example: clim**b** The tree was hard to climb.
    d) Example: desi**g**n The design of the house
       was amazing.
    e) Example: as**c**end She decided to ascend the
       tallest mountain.
    f) Example: ai**s**le They found the oranges in the
       fruit aisle.
2. a) knuckles b) sign c) answer d) wrist e) plumber

Page 53
Challenge 1
1. a) practice b) past c) banned d) father
Challenge 2
1. a) cereal b) herd c) aloud d) bridal
2. a) advice b) device c) wary d) proceed
Challenge 3
1. Each answer must use the given word correctly with
    a) showing an understanding that ascent means
    moving up, and b) showing an understanding that
    assent means agreement to or with something.
2. a) disagreeing with a decision or point of view
    b) something moving down (e.g. descending a
    mountain)

Page 55
Challenge 1
1. a) silly – 2; silliness – 1; sincere – 4; sinner – 6; sincerity
    – 5; since – 3
    b) wish – 5; wishful – 6; wash – 1; wise – 3; wisely – 4;
    wisdom – 2

Challenge 2

1. a) noun and verb
   b) noun and verb and adjective
   c) noun and verb
   d) adverb and adjective and verb and noun.
   e) verb and noun

Challenge 3

1. a) precede – come before something; verb
   b) proceed – begin something or move forward; verb
   c) principal – most important or leader; adjective and noun
   d) principle – a rule or truth; noun
   e) stationary – not moving; adjective
   f) stationery – writing and office materials; noun

Page 57

Challenge 1

1. a) A small child b) Teenager c) Somebody in charge of motor racing

Challenge 2

1. a) Instructions b) Information text c) Recount of events d) Newspaper report e) Fiction story

Challenge 3

1.

Story for four-year-old	Story for teacher
Examples: Simple ideas Simple language Pictures Shorter sentences	Examples: Wider range of grammatical features Literary techniques such as similes and metaphors More technical or complicated vocabulary

Page 59

Challenge 1

1.

Paragraph 1: The person	Paragraph 2: The painter
She was a kind lady. She was quiet and reserved. She enjoyed spending time in the countryside.	She painted trees and plants. She was a great artist. She used oil paints.

Challenge 2

1. The response must acknowledge the need to separate different ideas in the text into different paragraphs and identify the different ideas in each chosen paragraph.

Challenge 3

1. The response must include two paragraphs, with clear separate ideas. e.g. family, friends or school, hobbies.
2. The response must indicate an understanding that your own different ideas require separate paragraphs. You need to be able to explain that a new idea/theme needs a new paragraph.

Page 61

Challenge 1

1. a) Example: A classroom: colourful walls, bright and lively, chattering voices
   b) Example: A postman: bent with the weight of his sack, cheery smile, red-faced
   c) Example: The postman: calm and happy, gentle and kind

Challenge 2

1. a) Examples: soared; glided
   b) Example: swooped to the ground
   c) Example: green hills and dark, jagged mountains

Challenge 3

1. Each sentence must develop the setting, and not be just a 'list' of features. Example: An eerie mist clung to the rooftop and tower, as the silence was disturbed by a loud raven. The gate was open and as I approached the huge wooden door, the gravel path crunched beneath my feet. A long chain hung down and as I reached for it to ring the bell, the air grew cold. With a single, low ding of the bell, icicles appeared above me.

2. Each sentence must give information about the character and can include physical attributes as well as the kind and gentle characteristics. Example: With her tall slender frame and huge mass of hair on top of her head, Miss Jones looked quite something. If you saw her and heard her booming voice for the first time she might even seem scary. Her words, though, were always gentle. She was a kind teacher, encouraging and calm, loving and caring to all the children.

Page 63

Challenge 1

1. wich (which); carrys (carries); europe (Europe); famus (famous); citys (cities); paris (Paris); traval (travel); style. (style?); tikets (tickets); pounds (pounds.)

Challenge 2

1. a) Example: The blue sky and the warm sun made it a glorious day.
   b) Example: Sheltering from the rain, they managed to stay dry beneath the broad leaves of a huge tree.
   c) Example: The food was delicious and I thoroughly enjoyed the meal.

Challenge 3

1. Passage to be improved but still contain information referring to the train being 'posh' – nice beds, gold taps, expensive food. Example: It is a luxurious way to travel. A good sleep is guaranteed in the highly comfortable beds, after taking a wash in water from the sinks' gold taps. Appreciate the beautiful scenery passing by while enjoying exquisite food in the restaurant. While the tickets are expensive, a journey aboard this marvellous train is a delight.

Pages 64–67

Progress test 3: English

1. over – heat; un – related; dis – agreement; il – luminate
2. a) became a red carpet b) whoosh c) like an even closer, more magnificent sun d) glowing golden globe
3. a) verb and noun b) verb and noun c) verb and noun and adjective d) noun and verb
4. a) practice b) heard c) morning d) weather
5. Examples: a) A sketch or design, a first attempt at a piece of writing, to draw a plan or sketch, to compose a piece of writing b) Air passing through a gap c) A time of calm d) Part of something
6. a) **mis**spelled b) **re**appear c) **dis**own d) **de**form
7. a) ficti**tious**, noun to adjective b) par**tial**, noun to adjective c) vi**cious**, noun to adjective d) finan**cial**, noun to adjective

8. **a)** recount **b)** report **c)** story **d)** instructions
   e) persuasive text
9. Examples must include more detail but maintain the
   original idea. Examples:
   a) Dark and dusty, whatever the attic was hiding sent
   a chill down the spine.
   b) Bouncing off the road with an almost deafening
   sound, the rain was torrential.
   c) The squeals, screams and laughter gave away the
   enjoyment of the thrilling ride.
10. Examples must contain a correct prefix and a correctly
    constructed sentence. Examples:
    a) There was a **mis**understanding in the playground.
    b) She was completely **dis**satisfied with the food at the
    restaurant.
    c) My brother used to be very **un**kind to me when we
    were younger.
    d) My sister goes to the new **pre**school.
11. **a)** ○ **b)** F **c)** F **d)** ○ **e)** ○ **f)** F
12. The response should acknowledge that a fact
    can be proved, and an opinion can differ from
    person-to-person.
13. **a)** spoiled **b)** She will no longer be cleverest in her class.
    c) Example: Hetty was a spoiled girl who was arguing
    with her mum about doing her homework. Her mum
    tried to persuade her to do it but Hetty stormed off.

MATHS
Page 69
Challenge 1
1. **a)** 5   **b)** 10
2. **a)** $3\frac{1}{2}$ **b)** $3\frac{2}{3}$
3. **a)** 15   **b)** 32
4. **a)** $\frac{11}{15}$ circled **b)** $\frac{4}{5}$ circled **c)** $\frac{5}{12}$ circled
Challenge 2
1. **a)** $\frac{33}{5}$ **b)** $\frac{35}{8}$
2. **a)** $5\frac{3}{4}$ **b)** $3\frac{3}{8}$
3. Tom (Accept $\frac{5}{12}$)
Challenge 3
1. **a)** $\frac{36}{5}$ **b)** $4\frac{5}{6}$ **c)** $\frac{97}{12}$ **d)** $4\frac{3}{8}$
2. **a)** $\frac{13}{20}$ **b)** $\frac{13}{18}$
3. Nia, Tara, Beth (Accept $1\frac{1}{4}$, $1\frac{1}{8}$, $\frac{11}{12}$)

Page 71
Challenge 1
1. **a)** $\frac{5}{8}$ **b)** $\frac{11}{12}$ **c)** $\frac{9}{20}$
2. $\frac{5}{12}$
3. **a)** $\frac{8}{3} = 2\frac{2}{3}$ **b)** $\frac{4}{3} = 1\frac{1}{3}$, $\frac{10}{3} = 3\frac{1}{3}$, $\frac{6}{3} = 2$
Challenge 2
1. **a)** $\frac{9}{10}$ **b)** $\frac{9}{12}$ (= $\frac{3}{4}$) **c)** $\frac{2}{9}$
2. $\frac{3}{8}$
3. **a)** $\frac{9}{5} = 1\frac{4}{5}$ **b)** $\frac{15}{5} = 3$ **c)** $\frac{21}{5} = 4\frac{1}{5}$
Challenge 3
1. **a)** $\frac{13}{12} = 1\frac{1}{12}$ **b)** $\frac{19}{12} = 1\frac{7}{12}$ **c)** $\frac{4}{15}$

2. **a)** 3   **b)** 5   **c)** 13
3. **a)** $\frac{9}{8} = 1\frac{1}{8}$ **b)** $\frac{25}{6} = 4\frac{1}{6}$

Page 73
Challenge 1
1. **a)** 0.7 **b)** 0.2 **c)** 0.37 **d)** 0.93 **e)** 0.09
2. **a)** 0.5 **b)** 0.25 **c)** 0.2
3. 0.75 (kg)
Challenge 2
1. **a)** 0.08 **b)** 0.9 **c)** 0.29 **d)** 0.09 **e)** 0.439
2. **a)** 0.8 **b)** 0.05 **c)** 0.66
3. 0.83
Challenge 3
1. **a)** 0.73 **b)** 0.028 **c)** 0.807 **d)** 9.13 **e)** 0.79 **f)** 3.441
2. **a)** 0.55 **b)** 0.98 **c)** 0.08
3. An explanation that shows either:
   $1\frac{1}{1,000} = 1.001$ or $1.1 = 1\frac{1}{10}$

Page 75
Challenge 1
1. **a)** $\frac{3}{10}$ **b)** $\frac{7}{100}$ **c)** $\frac{9}{1,000}$ **d)** $\frac{39}{100}$ **e)** $\frac{19}{100}$ **f)** $\frac{437}{1,000}$
2. **a)** $\frac{1}{2}$ **b)** $\frac{1}{4}$ **c)** $\frac{3}{4}$
3. $\frac{1}{5}$
Challenge 2
1. **a)** $\frac{91}{100}$ **b)** $\frac{817}{1,000}$ **c)** $\frac{607}{1,000}$ **d)** $10\frac{1}{100}$ **e)** $\frac{97}{1,000}$ **f)** $\frac{777}{1,000}$
2. **a)** $(\frac{25}{1,000} =) \frac{1}{40}$ **b)** $(\frac{5}{100} =) \frac{1}{20}$ **c)** $(\frac{92}{100} =) \frac{23}{25}$
3. $4\frac{7}{10}$
Challenge 3
1. **a)** $(\frac{15}{100} =) \frac{3}{20}$ **b)** $(\frac{48}{100} =) \frac{12}{25}$ **c)** $(\frac{85}{100} =) \frac{17}{20}$
   d) $(\frac{52}{100} =) \frac{13}{25}$ **e)** $(\frac{75}{1,000} =) \frac{3}{40}$ **f)** $(\frac{125}{1,000} =) \frac{1}{8}$
2. **a)** $(6\frac{6}{10} =) 6\frac{3}{5}$ **b)** $(10\frac{95}{100} =) 10\frac{19}{20}$ **c)** $(8\frac{16}{100} =) 8\frac{4}{25}$
   d) $(3\frac{125}{1,000} =) 3\frac{1}{8}$ **e)** $(9\frac{72}{100} =) 9\frac{18}{25}$ **f)** $(2\frac{375}{1,000} =) 2\frac{3}{8}$
3. 0.52

Page 77
Challenge 1
1. **a)** 6   **b)** 11
2. **a)** 5.6 > 5.27 **b)** 14.8 > 1.48
3. Maria (Accept 73.5 cm)
Challenge 2
1. **a)** 12 **b)** 20
2. **a)** 7.1 **b)** 25.6
3. **a)** 5.16   5.61   6.15   6.51
   b) 68.078   68.708   68.807   68.87
4. Josh (Accept £12.76)
Challenge 3
1. **a)** 40 **b)** 25
2. **a)** 12.0 **b)** 52.2
3. **a)** 6.245   6.254   6.452   6.542
   b) 11.018   11.081   11.1   11.18
4. Tia (Accept 14.149 (seconds))

Page 79
Challenge 1

1. ✓

2. a) $\frac{29}{100}$ b) $\frac{87}{100}$ c) $\frac{43}{100}$
3. a) 0.67 b) 0.09 c) 0.99
4. 30 (pupils)
Challenge 2
1. 16 (sections)
2. a) $\frac{3}{5}$ b) $\frac{7}{10}$ c) $\frac{3}{4}$ d) $\frac{1}{20}$
3. a) 57% b) 7% c) 30%
4. £12
Challenge 3
1. a) $\left(\frac{15}{100}=\right)\frac{3}{20}$, 0.15
   b) $\left(\frac{90}{100}=\right)\frac{9}{10}$, 0.9
2. 42 (minutes)   3. £18   4. £30

Page 81
Challenge 1
1. a) 5 (m) b) 5 (litres) c) 6,000 (g) d) 7,000 (m) e) 50 (cm)
2. a) 6 (minutes)   b) 4 (weeks)   c) 240 (minutes)
3. 3rd May   4. 50 minutes
Challenge 2
1. a) 6.3 (m) b) 8.3 (litres) c) 9,600 (g) d) 7,250 (m)
   e) 250 (ml)
2. a) 330 (seconds)   b) 168 (hours)   c) 450 (minutes)
3. 2 hours 30 minutes   4. 8th April
Challenge 3
1. a) 97.5 (m) b) 10,200 (ml) c) 12,750 (m) d) 750 (g)
   e) 5.05 (kg)
2. $3\frac{1}{2}$ hours (Accept 210 minutes)   3. Sunday

Page 83
Accept slight variations in answers if different conversion methods have been used.
Challenge 1
1. a) 12.5 (centimetres) b) 27 (litres) c) 1.35 (grams)
2. 45 (cm)   3. 450 (g)   4. 13.5 (litres)
Challenge 2
1. a) 10.8 (metres) b) 40.5 (litres) c) 1,800 (grams)
2. 36 (metres) 3. 5.5 (pounds)   4. 105 (centimetres)
Challenge 3
1. a) 12.5 (centimetres) b) 27 (litres) c) 3.6 (kilograms)
2. a) 150 (centimetres) b) 25.2 (kilograms)
3. 67.5 (litres)   4. 1,300 (grams)

Page 85
Challenge 1
1. a) 32 cm   b) 48 cm²
2. a) 64 cm³ b) 27 cm³
Challenge 2
1. a) Perimeter = 74 cm   Area = 195 cm²
   b) Perimeter = 60 cm   Area = 190 cm²
2. 8 cm long, 7 cm wide underlined
   10 cm long, 2 cm wide ticked
Challenge 3
1. 1 litre
2. a) 14 cm   b) 5 cm
3. 180 cm

Page 87
Challenge 1
1. £12.65   2. 850 m or 0.85 km
3. 3,600 g or 3.6 kg   4. 250 ml or 0.25 litres
Challenge 2
1. £81.35 2. 2.55 m 3. 575 g 4. 8 (bottles) 5. £56.25
Challenge 3
1. a) 9 (eggs) b) 36 (cupcakes)
2. a) 3.05 kg or 3,050 g   b) 3.1 kg or 3,100 g
   (Accept a correct calculation of 6.15 kg minus an
   incorrect answer in Q2a)
3. £66

Pages 88–91
Progress test 4: maths
1. a) 619,907 b) 121,688   121,788
2. a) 53 b) 109 c) 444 d) 1990
3. a) 545 b) 137 c) 424
4. a) 2,702   b) 10,014
5. a) 480 b) 19   c) 60
6. a) $\frac{2}{5} = \frac{4}{10} = \frac{6}{15} = \frac{8}{20} = \frac{10}{25}$
   b) $\frac{3}{8} = \frac{15}{40}$ c) $\frac{5}{12} = \frac{20}{48}$
7. a) $\left(\frac{75}{100}=\right)\frac{3}{4}$ b) $\frac{3}{10}$ c) $\frac{9}{100}$ d) 0.7 e) 0.53 f) 0.009
8. a) £15 b) £7.50
9. a) 7 (metres)   b) 0.8 (kilograms)   c) 5 (litres)
10. 150 m²
11. 53,568   53,856   53,865   54,368   54,865
12. Accept any 5-digit number with digits placed as shown:
    2*,7*4
13. a) 52,890   b) 53,000   c) 50,000
14. 428 (oranges)
15. a) 9   b) 40
16. 20 (°C)
17. a) 765 b) 1,238
18. a) 44.7 (kilometres per hour)
    b) 45 (kilometres per hour)
19. 2 hours 55 minutes 20. 450 (litres)
21. a) −4   b) 2   c) −1
22. a) £122.50 b) £1,225
23. a) 31,716   b) 113,886
24. $\frac{1}{2}$ $\frac{13}{24}$ $\frac{7}{12}$ $\frac{5}{8}$ $\frac{2}{3}$ (Accept $\frac{12}{24}$ $\frac{13}{24}$ $\frac{14}{24}$ $\frac{15}{24}$ $\frac{16}{24}$)
25. £2
26. 266 (metres)
27. 3,750 + 2,984 = 6,734
28. a) 100 b) 729 c) 225
29. 0.689 kg   0.69 kg   0.696 kg   0.7 kg   0.703 kg
30. 71   73   79   all circled
31. 390 (supporters)   32. 5 (pieces)   33. 2
34. 840 cm³   35. 1,365 mm or 1.365 m   36. £3,750
37. 30.8 (litres) 38. 19,416 (people)

ENGLISH
Page 93
Challenge 1
1. a) The car, that was old and noisy, stopped.
   b) Gran, who plays golf each week, got a hole in one.
   c) I have a big teddy, which I won in a raffle.
   d) This is the painting that everyone is talking about.
   e) There are the children who climbed over the fence.
2. a) the car b) Gran c) a teddy d) the painting
   e) the children

Challenge 2

1. **a)** who **b)** whose **c)** which **d)** where **e)** that

Challenge 3

1. Sentences to make sense and start with the correct relative pronoun. Examples:
   a) who looks after people. **b)** that has a lovely café. **c)** which I love **d)** that flooded the street **e)** which came from the attic.

Page 95

Challenge 1

1. **a)** possibly **b)** Perhaps **c)** surely **d)** definitely
2. **a)** Certain to happen ✓ **b)** Not certain to happen ✓ **c)** Certain to happen ✓ **d)** Not certain to happen ✓

Challenge 2

1. **a)** could **b)** would **c)** can **d)** must **e)** might **f)** should

Challenge 3

1. Examples: **a)** Maybe/Perhaps **b)** surely/definitely **c)** definitely/certainly **d)** Perhaps/Maybe
2. Each modal verb must make sense in the sentence. Examples: **a)** should **b)** can **c)** could **d)** will

Page 97

Challenge 1

1. **a)** played **b)** jumped **c)** works **d)** eats
2. Examples: **a)** We play football in the garden.
   b) Everybody was/will be jumping on the bouncy castle when it was/is ready.
   c) She is/was/will be working hard to improve her running pace.
   d) He ate breakfast before he got dressed.

Challenge 2

1. **a)** He jumped over the wall and twisted his ankle. OR He jumps over the wall and twists his ankle.
   b) She entered the competition and won first prize. OR She enters the competition and wins first prize.
   c) They walk along the path and arrive at a dead end. OR They walked along the path and arrived at a dead end.

Challenge 3

1. Accept reasonable sentences with verbs consistently in the future tense. Example: I am going to go to the moon. When I get there, I will take photographs and work in a space base. The views will be amazing and I'll enjoy the trip.
2. Accept reasonable sentences with verbs consistently in the past tense. Example: I went to the moon. When I got there, I took photographs and worked in a space base. The views were amazing and I enjoyed the trip.

Page 99

Challenge 1

1. **a)** At lunchtime **b)** Before **c)** then **d)** During

Challenge 2

1. Eden and Dev walked to the lake. Before long, they paddled in the water. Next, they started skimming stones. Eden was great at this because her mum had told her what to do.
   Later, they called Dev's dad to pick them up. After a few minutes, he arrived in his car.
2. Example: During the afternoon, they called Dev's dad to pick them up. Moments later, he arrived in his car.

Challenge 3

1. A variety of possibilities. Ensure the writing makes sense and is correctly punctuated. Example: The car was dirty. During the journey, Dev said that it had not been cleaned for months. **Suddenly**, Dev's dad had an idea. He told Eden and Dev they could clean the car. **Soon**, they were home. **Later**, Dev's dad got out the bucket and the hosepipe.

Page 101

Challenge 1

1. **a)** First **b)** Next **c)** Before lunch **d)** During the afternoon **e)** Later on

Challenge 2

1. quickly; after the downpour; Inside the house; Soon; Later on

Challenge 3

1. Examples: **Soon** they could see more details. **Slowly**, the boat approached the lights. **By now** the bedraggled crew… **Finally**, the boat managed to dock.

Page 103

Challenge 1

1. **a)** Tilly had pizza, chips and milkshake at the party.
   b) The children played ball, skipping and hopping games.
   c) It was Kenji's birthday and he had cakes, ice cream and jelly for tea.
   d) Stella enjoyed reading, writing and picture books.
2. Each list must be separated by commas and use 'and' or 'or' after the penultimate word. Examples:
   a) Emma, Emily, Emmie or Emile.
   b) history, art, English and maths.
   c) bread, milk, cheese and butter.
   d) Argentina, Croatia, Japan and Norway.

Challenge 2

1. **a)** "Hurry up and hide, Jack," said Lisa.
   b) "Can we bake, Grandma?" asked the children.
   c) Most of the time, travellers take a taxi from the airport.
   d) Sam likes his friends, playing computer games and football.

Challenge 3

1. Answers should refer to:
   a) removing ambiguity by showing that Lisa is telling Jack to hide, rather than telling someone else to hide Jack.
   b) removing ambiguity by showing that the children are addressing/asking Grandma, rather than wanting to bake her.
   c) removing ambiguity to show the sentence is not about time travellers.
   d) Removing ambiguity by showing that the sentence contains a list of things Sam likes (rather than liking his friends playing computer games).

Page 105

Challenge 1

1. **a)** My sisters (both netball players) go to college.
   b) The team played really well (scoring two goals) and won the game.

c) We ordered a lot from the takeaway (we were really hungry!).

d) Betty and Jim (from London) won the contest.

2. a) The house <u>that has just been built</u> is enormous.

b) Roisin had a pony <u>that had a long mane</u>.

c) The old man <u>who works in the shop</u> is very kind.

d) The test <u>that I spent hours revising for</u> was cancelled.

Challenge 2

1. a) Jenny's parents, who are doctors, work at the hospital.

b) The car, which won the race last year, is up for sale.

c) Kelly, who plays for the rugby team, got a medal for good training.

d) Danny's grandad, who writes stories, was on television.

2. a) ✓ b) ✗ c) ✗ d) ✓ e) ✗

Challenge 3

1. The traffic, usually busy at this time, was moving well.

Rosie (the best dancer in the class) was amazing.

Evan – stylish and chatty as ever – made everybody laugh.

Pages 106–109

Progress test 5: English

1. Each word must be included in a grammatically correct sentence. Examples:

a) care<u>ful</u>; They were careful when balancing on the edge of the roof.

b) <u>re</u>appear; They had been waiting for the wizard to reappear.

c) <u>dis</u>like; For some reason, she had a strong dislike of this place.

d) slow<u>ly</u>; It was slowly getting lighter.

2. a) On the trip were Ben, Naz and Jess.

b) We ate cheese, crisps and chicken nuggets at the party.

c) Milly's three hobbies are painting, sailing boats and swimming.

d) Everyone heard the fizz, whoosh and bang of the firework.

3. Examples: a) He crawled along as slowly as a snail.

b) Her angry stare was as cold as ice.

c) The paper drifted into the sky like a majestic eagle.

d) The variety of food was colourful like a rainbow.

4. a) wid**en** b) just**ify** c) medic**ate** d) real**ise** e) solid**ify** f) hard**en** g) alien**ate** h) class**ify**

5. Responses must make sense and relate to the context. Examples:

a) turbulent / swirling

b) storm clouds / clouds gathering.

c) thrown / tossed

6. a) Ciara's new ball <u>that bounces really high</u> was a present from Tom.

b) Seb<u>, who goes to gym club,</u> can do somersaults.

c) Ged has a dog<u>, which he walks twice a day.</u>

d) The new house <u>where James lives</u> is very nice.

7. a) couldn't/could not

b) will or can or should or must

c) will or can or should or could

d) should or must or will

8. a) Kelly **smiled** and then **ate** all the ice cream.

b) We **played** netball and **won**.

c) They **ran** fast and **finished** first in the relay race.

d) She **drew** a picture and **showed** it to Mum.

e) He **danced** at the disco and **had** a great time.

f) Milly **baked** a cake and **sold** it to her gran.

9. a) Henry VIII (an English king) had six wives.

b) We went to Paris (the capital of France) for the weekend.

c) The house (probably haunted) had been in their family for centuries.

d) Ella and Jack (my cousins) won the singing competition.

10. a) burnt branches, brambles and bush – alliteration

crackle of flames – onomatopoeia

a blanket over everything – metaphor

cunning as a fox – simile

b) The response should acknowledge that it appears that life in the woodland was destroyed by fire but Joe is looking for hope in the form of new life growing there.

11. a) Opinion b) Fact c) Opinion d) Opinion e) Fact f) Fact

12. a) anxious b) official c) infectious d) partial

13. a) The response should indicate an upbeat, happy voice.

b) trees c) strange d) such a splendid sound

e) young children

14. a) <u>k</u>nowledge, Example: His knowledge of birds is extraordinary.

b) cal<u>f</u>, Example: When the calf was born it was weak.

c) comb, Example: I comb my hair ten times a day.

d) <u>w</u>rong, Example: I was upset that I got the answer wrong.

MATHS

Page 111

Challenge 1

1. a) 11 cm b) 9 cm

2. a) 7 cm b) 10 cm

3. ▱ circled

Challenge 2

1. a) 10 cm b) 38 cm c) 26 cm d) 15 cm e) 7 cm f) 20 cm

Challenge 3

1. a) 5.5 cm b) 72 cm c) 28.5 cm d) 7 cm e) 20 cm f) 180 cm

2. An explanation that shows that although rhombuses have 4 equal sides, not all rhombuses have equal angles. (Accept a drawing that indicates a rhombus with unequal angles.)

Page 113

Challenge 1

1. a) cuboid

b) triangular-based pyramid (Accept tetrahedron)

c) pentagonal prism

2. a) 6 b) 5 c) 6

Challenge 2

1. a) cube b) cylinder c) hexagonal prism

2. a) triangular (prism) b) hexagonal-based (pyramid)

Challenge 3

1. a) 8 (faces), 18 (edges), 12 (vertices)

b) 10 (faces), 24 (edges), 16 (vertices)

2. a) [net diagram] b) [net diagram] c) [net diagram]

Page 115

Challenge 1

1. B D A E C
2. B ✓ D ✓

Challenge 2

1. 178° 98° both circled
2. a) 52° b) 93°
3. a) 22° b) 193°

Challenge 3

1. a) 81° b) 73°
2. 22.5° 3. 59°
4. An explanation that shows that either
   all numbers <90 added to numbers >90 but <180 do
   not always give a total >180. OR gives a counter-
   example, e.g. 1° + 91° = 92° and 92° is an obtuse angle
   or is not a reflex angle.

Page 117

Challenge 1

1. d) ✓
2.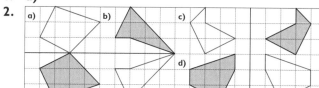

Challenge 2   **Challenge 3**

1.   1.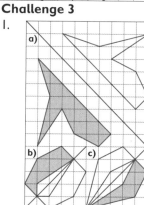

Page 119

Challenge 1

1.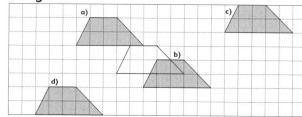

Challenge 2

1. a) 4 left, 2 down b) 12 right, 4 down c) 2 left, 5 up
   d) 16 left, 2 up

Challenge 3

1. a) (7, 12)   (7, 16)   (11, 12)   (11, 16)
   b) (15, 6)   (15, 10)   (19, 6)   (19, 10)
   c) (9, 3)   (9, 7)   (13, 3)   (13, 7)
   d) (12, 14)   (12, 18)   (16, 14)   (16, 18)

Page 121

Challenge 1

1. 58 minutes
2. Durham
3. 10:18 (Accept 10:18 to 10:48 or 30 minutes or 2nd train)
4. 744 (men)

Challenge 2

1. 23 minutes 2. 28 minutes 3. 12:45 4. 152 (women)

Challenge 3

1. 38 minutes 2. 1 hour 52 minutes 3. 36 (children)
4. An explanation that shows not all people will stay on
   the train and people may get off (at Northallerton,
   Darlington and Durham) and / or other people may
   get on the train.

Page 123

Challenge 1

1. 8 kg 2. 12 kg 3. 4 kg 4. February

Challenge 2

1. 3 kg
2. 7 kg   (Accept any mass from ≧6.5 kg to ≦7.5 kg)
3. 8 kg
4. Accept any date from 20th August to 1st September
   inclusive.

Challenge 3

1. Accept any answer from >4.5 months to <5.5 months.
2. Accept any answer from >5.5 months to <6.5 months.
3. Accept any mass from ≧2.75 kg to ≦3.25 kg
4. Accept any answer from ≧4.25 months to ≦4.75 months.

Pages 124–127

Progress test 6: maths

1. a) 4,899 b) 8,017 c) 4,217
2. a) b)
3. a) 4 (kg) b) 3,500 (ml) c) 12.5 (m)
4. a) 360 cm² b) 144 cm²
5. 11.25 litres or 11,250 ml
6. a) triangular prism b) pentagonal-based pyramid
7. 148,357 circled
8. 17 9. 3.25 (kg) 10. 50 (m)
11.
12. a) 133 b) 103,302
13. 318 (tickets) 14. Leo   (Accept $\frac{5}{12}$ or $\frac{20}{48}$)
15. a) 40 b) 39.7
16. a) 42° b) 309°
17. a) 62 (pears) b) 36 (bananas) c) 45 (bananas)
18.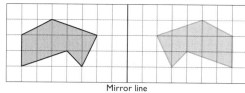

Mirror line

19. a) 2 hours, 22 minutes b) 12:15
    c) 12:15 (Accept 12:15 to 14:27 or 2 hours 12 minutes
    or 4th train)
20. 16.94   16.934   16.08   15.9   15.831
21. 84 cm 22. 45°
23.

24. 12°

25. a) March and April **b)** November
   c) Accept any answer $\geqq$85 mm to $\leqq$86 mm
   d) Accept any answer $\geqq$25 mm to $\leqq$29 mm

Pages 128–134
Mixed questions: English

1. a) Facts: There were 19,202 people in the stadium.; James Trent scored 2 goals.; United are now top of the league.
   Opinion: Everybody wanted to watch this football match.; He will soon be the best player in the country.; Everyone will be happy with that.
   b) Example: There were 19,202 people – this is a fact because they will have been counted when they entered the stadium.
   c) Example: Everybody wanted to watch this football match – this is opinion as it is likely that there are some people who did not want to watch the match.

2. belief – 2; believe – 4; believer – 5; believable – 3; believing – 6; belie – 1

3. a) The response should indicate a quiet, sad, slow or sorrowful voice (any combination of these).
   b) The response could indicate that it is about holding back tears, holding on to somebody, or holding on to memories.
   c) The response should indicate that the word is repeated to show that the holding is ongoing or that it is hard to let go.
   d) There is a 'wish' that things could change.

4. a) "It's time to get chopping, children," said Dad with an axe in his hand.
   b) There was juggling, a man on stilts and a clown at the circus entrance.

5. villige – village; distanse – distance; vally – valley; a – an; river – river.; it. – it?; their – there; now – know; whith – with; advencher – adventure

6. a) allowed **b)** advice **c)** guessed **d)** precede

7. Accept examples that are grammatically correct and use the given word correctly. Examples:
   a) It was a pleasing end to the day.
   b) They took great pleasure from their pets.
   c) He was very displeased that the letter had not arrived.
   d) The loud music was a most unpleasurable experience.

8. a) attend **b)** hear **c)** equal **d)** rely

9. Sentences should be grammatically correct and should use the given word correctly. Examples:
   a) colum<u>n</u> The statue was on a tall column.
   b) recei<u>p</u>t They kept the receipt in case the gift needed to be returned.
   c) mus<u>c</u>le She pulled a muscle playing rugby.
   d) s<u>c</u>ene Before them was a beautiful scene.
   e) <u>w</u>reck The diver discovered the wreck at a depth of 30 metres.

10.

Paragraph 1: The car	Paragraph 2: The race
a blue and red racing car; a large number 7 on the roof; the fastest car; a powerful engine	fast and furious as the cars sped along; the growl of several engines; a crash and pile up; the crowd cheered

11. a) where **b)** that **c)** which **d)** where

12. Each response must have at least one definition.
   father – a male parent, noun; to father a child, verb
   farther – a greater distance, adverb
   descent – moving downwards, noun
   decent – good, acceptable, adjective
   steal – to take something belonging to someone else, verb; something bought cheaply, noun
   steel – strong metal (or alloy), noun; to steel oneself, verb

13. a) peacefully **b)** angrily **c)** daily **d)** nearby

14. b)✓ **d)**✓

15. a) baked **b)** swimming **c)** cook **d)** saw

16. a) Any four from: costumes; dancing; acting; music; singing; stunts
   b) the music and singing were a shining light
   c) action at great heights and nerve-wracking balancing
   d) The answer should make reference to the first paragraph being about the musical in general, with the second paragraph focusing on the stunts.

17. a) Example: Fact – My mum works in a bank.
   b) Example: Opinion – Mr Smith is the best teacher in the world.

18. The summary should be of a familiar story with the three sentences covering the main detail.
   Example: The mouse is looking for a nut to eat. The other creatures in the wood seem to want to eat the mouse, and so does the Gruffalo. The mouse tricks the other creatures and the Gruffalo into thinking he is brave and strong.

19. a) stars like diamonds
   b) She must be a very good rower because she has been rowing for several hours (and could do more).
   c) The two paragraphs contain different ideas/aspects of the story. The first is about the character rowing and enjoying the calm. The second paragraph is about a creature beneath the boat.
   d) The response must include a reason. Example: The creature attacks the boat and the character and her dog face a battle to survive. It seems that the creature is going to attack and the text has so much calm in it to begin with, and this calm is ready to be broken.

20. a) weary **b)** guest **c)** passed **d)** dessert

21. a) Any two from: Moments later; Later that day; Suddenly **b)** … like a proud statue. **c)** Any two from: excitedly; completely; Suddenly; tightly **d)** past tense
   e) She is nervous and a bit frightened about seeing the lion. Evidence includes, 'I gasped. He was so big.' and that she hid behind Mum.
   f) Any reasonable answer. Example: Mum and Sophie cannot find Freddie. He has run off ahead again and got lost in the crowds.

22. a) thumb **b)** knocked **c)** numb **d)** scissors **e)** plumber
   f) ghost

23. a) Examples: My name is Jon. I have brown hair.
   b) Examples: My house is the nicest one on the street. My cat is the cutest cat in the world.

Pages 135–143
Mixed questions: maths

1. a) 12,730 **b)** 131,080   130,080
   c) 250,600   240,600   230,600

2. a) III **b)** 2,880 **c)** 449

3. 188

4. a) 0.4 **b)** 0.73 **c)** 0.07 **d)** 0.006 **e)** 0.203

5. £33.18

6. a) Accept any answer ≧13.5 °C to ≦14.5 °C
   b) 4 (Saturdays)
   c) Accept any answer ≧9.5 °C to ≦10.5 °C

7. 3   4   12   15   20   all circled

8. Manchester Stoke Coventry Sunderland Preston
   (Accept 395,515   372,775   359,262   335,415
   313,332)

9. a) $\left(\frac{4}{12} =\right) \frac{1}{3}$ **b)** $\left(\frac{17}{15} =\right) 1\frac{2}{15}$ **c)** $\frac{13}{20}$

10.

	Length	Width	Perimeter	Area
a)	12 cm	8 cm	**40 cm**	**96 cm²**
b)	30 cm	20 cm	**100 cm**	**600 cm²**
c)	**9 cm**	7 cm	32 cm	63 cm²
d)	**5 cm**	**5 cm**	20 cm	25 cm²

11.

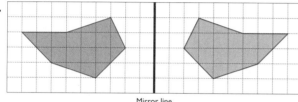

Mirror line

12. Manisha and her mother are both correct because
   $\frac{6}{12} = \frac{1}{2}$

13. 48 (questions correct)

14. 1912

15. a) 4,013 **b)** 7,312

16. square circled

17. 1,775 g or 1.775 kg

18. a) 32,814 (males) **b)** 12,249 (people) **c)** 782

19. 4 days 5 hours

20. a) 144 **b)** 1,000 **c)** 100

21. 0.5 (kg)

22.

fraction		decimal		percentage
$\frac{3}{4}$	=	**0.75**	=	**75%**
$\frac{4}{5}$	=	**0.8**	=	80%
$\frac{19}{20}$	=	0.95	=	**95%**

23. seven thousand circled

24. 30 litres

25.

26. a) 109,000 **b)** 100,000 **c)** 110,000 **d)** 109,050

27. a) **6,952** + 2,091 = 9,043
   b) 87,541 − 4,827 = **82,714** (Accept 87,541 − **82,714** =
   4,827)

28. 53   59

29. Beth   (Accept $\frac{3}{10}$ or $\frac{6}{20}$)

30. length = 90 m   width = 72 m (Accept different
   acceptable methods for converting yards to metres,)

31. a) 7.039   7.093   7.903   7.93
   b) 16.695   16.965   17.86   17.865

32. An explanation that shows either: regular shapes
   must have equal angles as well as equal sides OR the
   decagon / star has angles of different sizes.

33. a) Accept any answer ≧4.5 °C to ≦5.5 °C
   b) Accept any answer ≧5.5 °C to ≦6.5 °C
   c) Accept any answer ≧4 hours to ≦4 hours 30 minutes
   d) Accept any answer ≧12 °C to ≦13 °C

34. a) 39° **b)** 102° **c)** 39° **d)** 202°

35. 23 °C

36. a) 11.54 **b)** 11:18 (Accept 4ᵗʰ train) **c)** 35 minutes
   d) 14:18

37. (0, 17)

38.

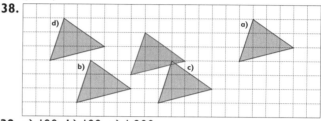

39. a) 100 **b)** 100 **c)** 1,000

40. 14 km

41. a) 3 **b)** 6 **c)** 2 **d)** 4 **e)** 5

42. a) 0.07 **b)** 0.009 **c)** 0.509 **d)** 50 **e)** 2.09 **f)** 7.345

43. a) 1.63 m   1.645 m   1.708 m   1.71 m   1.784 m
   b) 1 (car) **c)** 2 (cars)

44. 3 hours 45 minutes (Accept $3\frac{3}{4}$ hours or 225 minutes)

45.

	Length	Width	Perimeter	Area
a)	12 cm	**12 cm**	48 cm	**144 cm²**
b)	**10 cm**	9 cm	**38 cm**	90 cm²
c)	20 cm	**10 cm**	60 cm	**200 cm²**
d)	**20 cm**	6 cm	**52 cm**	120 cm²
e)	25 cm	**6 cm**	62 cm	**150 cm²**

46.

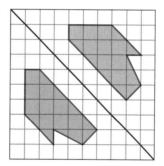

47. a) 6,814 − 1,259 **b)** 7,355 + 1,883
   c) 435 × 26 = 2,610 + 8,700 **d)** 803 × 57

48. £96.86   **49.** −11   **50. a)** 22° **b)** 79°

51. −3

52. 24 (Accept any multiple of 24)   **53.** $\frac{7}{12}$

Maths glossary

2-D Describes shapes that have only two dimensions: length and width (or breadth).

3-D Describes shapes that have three dimensions: length, width (or breadth) and height. These shapes exist in the real world and if small enough, can be handled.

Acute angle An angle that is smaller than a right angle and so has less than 90°.

Addition An operation to find the total of two or more numbers.

Angle A turn around a point. Angles are measured in degrees.

Apex The top or highest part of a shape.

Area The amount of space inside a 2-D shape. It is measured using square units such as square centimetres (cm^2) or square metres (m^2).

Capacity The space taken up by a 3-D shape or object. It is usually used to describe how much liquid an object can hold and measured in millilitres and litres.

Common factor Because 4 is a factor of 20 and it is also a factor of 36, so 4 is a common factor of 20 and 36. Other common factors of 24 and 36 are 1, 2, 3, (4), 6, 12. 12 is the largest common factor and so is the **highest/ greatest common factor**.

Common multiple If a number is a multiple of two or more numbers then it is a common multiple of these numbers: 24 is a common multiple of 4 and 6. 12 would be the **lowest common multiple** of 4 and 6

Composite number A number that can be made by multiplying two whole numbers as well as itself and 1

Composite rectilinear shape A shape made up of two or more rectangles.

Cube number The result of multiplying a number by itself twice. So, $3 \times 3 \times 3 = 27$, 27 is a cube number. $3 \times 3 \times 3$ can be written as 3^3 (say 'three cubed'). Here the index is 3, so three 3s are multiplied.

Cubic centimetres Cubes that have a unit measure, so a cubic centimetre has sides of 1 centimetre.

Cubic metres Cubes that have a unit measure, so a cubic metre has sides of 1 metre.

Decimal Our number system is based on groups of ten (decimal means counting in tens). All commonly used numbers are decimal numbers but usually decimals or decimal numbers refer to numbers with a **decimal point**.

Decimal place (dp) Describes the position of a digit used in a number to the right of the decimal point. The first digit after the decimal point has the first decimal place, the second has the second decimal place and so on.

Decimal point Like a full stop, used in decimal numbers to separate whole numbers from parts of whole numbers, e.g. $43\frac{7}{10} = 43.7$

Degrees The units used to measure a turn. There are 360° in a full turn.

Denominator The number below the dividing line in a fraction; shows the number of parts the whole is divided into, e.g. in $\frac{3}{4}$ the whole is divided into four parts.

Diagonal A line that joins the corners (vertices) of a 2-D or 3-D shape but is not the side of a 2-D shape or the edge of a 3-D shape.

Division Sharing a number into equal groups, e.g. dividing by 4 shares the number into four equal groups, e.g. $16 \div 4 = 4$, there are four equal groups of 4. Also a way of counting back in steps and knowing the number of backward steps, e.g. $8 \div 3 = 2 \ r \ 2$

Equivalent fraction Fractions that have the same value, e.g. $\frac{2}{5} = \frac{4}{10} = \frac{6}{15} = \frac{8}{20}$

Factor A number that is multiplied to get another number, e.g. $4 \times 5 = 20$, so 4 and 5 are factors of 20

Factor pairs For most numbers, factors come in pairs as two numbers are multiplied together. So, the factor pairs for 20 would be: 1 and 20, 2 and 10, 4 and 5, sometimes, these would be written as 1×20, 2×10, 4×5

Fraction When a whole is divided into equal parts, each part is a fraction of the whole. The whole can vary. It may be, e.g. 18 kg, a square or 24. A fraction is one number made up of two parts: the numerator above the dividing line and the denominator below.

Frequency table Records how often something happens.

Improper fraction A fraction that represents numbers that are a whole or are greater than a whole, e.g. $\frac{5}{5}$ would be a whole. $\frac{6}{5}$ is greater than one whole.

Imperial measures An older system of measures used for many years before **metric measures**. They include inches, feet, yards and miles (length), ounces, pounds and stones (mass) and pints and gallons (capacity).

Index (plural: indices) A number written to the upper right of another number, e.g. 4^3. The number three is the index. It tells you how many times the number should be multiplied together, so, $4^3 = 4 \times 4 \times 4$

Inverse An operation that reverses another operation, e.g. subtraction is the inverse of addition; division is the inverse of multiplication.

Irregular Describes a 2-D shape that does not have equal sides or equal angles.

Line graph A graph that shows a line or lines that display continuous information, often over a period of time.

Long multiplication A written method of completing multiplication, often with larger numbers set out in columns. It records each individual multiplication of each pair of digits.

Lowest terms   When a fraction is reduced to its lowest terms, it means the digits used are as small as possible, e.g. here is a set of equivalent fractions: $\frac{2}{5} = \frac{4}{10} = \frac{6}{15} = \frac{8}{20}$ so $\frac{8}{20}$ in its lowest terms is $\frac{2}{5}$

Metric measures   A system of measures based on groups of 10 units. The basic units are metre (length), kilogram (mass) and litre (capacity).

Mirror line   The line of reflection; the line over which a shape is flipped so it can be reflected.

Mixed number   A whole number written with a fraction, e.g. $\frac{6}{5} = 1\frac{1}{5}$

Multiplication   A way of making repeated additions, e.g. $4 \times 3 = 4 + 4 + 4 = 12$

Multiple   The answer when two whole numbers are multiplied, e.g. $4 \times 6 = 24$, so 24 is a multiple of 4 and 6

Negative number   A number less than zero, e.g. negative seven or -7 is seven less than zero.

Notation   The way numbers are written down by using a set of symbols, e.g. 1, 2, 3

Numerator   The number above the dividing line in a fraction; shows the number of parts being dealt with, e.g. $\frac{3}{4}$ – there are three parts needed.

Oblong   A rectangle that is not a square.

Obtuse angle   An angle larger than a right angle, more than 90°, but smaller than a straight angle, less than 180°.

Operation   A mathematical process; the most common are addition, subtraction, multiplication and division.

Parallel   Lines that are always the same distance apart.

Percentage (%)   A special type of fraction that shows the number of parts per hundred or as hundredths, e.g. 23% = 23 out of 100 = $\frac{23}{100}$

Perimeter   The length of the outside edge of a shape. It is a length and is usually measured in centimetres (cm) or metres (m).

Place holder   A digit used to make sure another digit appears in the correct column, e.g. 300, there are two zeros to make sure the digit 3 is in the hundreds column. The zeros are the place holders.

Place value   The value of a digit according to its position in a number, e.g. in the number 285, the digit 8 has a place value of eight tens or 80, because it is in the tens column.

Polygon   Any 2-D shape with straight sides.

Powers of 10   Numbers achieved by multiplying 10 by itself twice or more, e.g. $10 \times 10 = 100$ and $10 \times 10 \times 10 = 1,000$. 100 and 1,000 are powers of 10

Prime number   A number that is greater than 1 that cannot be made by multiplying two whole numbers together apart from multiplying by 1 and the number itself, e.g. 11 has no other factors than 1 and 11

Prime factor   A factor that is a prime number, e.g. 3 is a factor of 15 and 3 is a prime number, so it is a prime factor.

Proper fraction   A fraction with a numerator that is less than the denominator, e.g. $\frac{3}{8}$ or $\frac{9}{10}$

Quadrilateral   A polygon with four sides.

Rate   A comparison of two related measurements or amounts, e.g. 3 apples for £1.60 or 100 ml of disinfectant for every 2 litres of water.

Rectangle   A 2-D shape; a quadrilateral with equal and opposite sides with 4 right angles.

Reflection   A shape viewed as if in a mirror; it has been flipped over.

Reflex angle   An angle greater than a straight angle, so has more than 180°.

Regular   Describes a 2-D shape with equal sides and equal angles.

Right angle   An angle of 90°. It is a quarter turn.

Scale   Used on maps and in model-making where one unit of measurement represents another unit, e.g. 1 centimetre represents 2 kilometres.

Short division   A written method of division that allows for mental calculation of remainders.

Square   A special kind of rectangle with four equal sides.

Square centimetre   Squares that have a unit measure, so a square centimetre has sides of 1 centimetre.

Square metre   Squares that have a unit measure, so a square metre has sides of 1 metre.

Square number   The result of multiplying a number by itself. So, $3 \times 3 = 9$, 9 is a square number. 3×3 can be written as 3^2 ('three squared'). 9 is the square number.

Straight angle   An angle where the turn causes one direction to become the opposite direction. It appears as a straight line. There are 180° in a straight angle.

Subtraction   An operation that takes one or more numbers away from another to find the difference.

Translation   The movement of a shape horizontally or vertically. As the shape moves, it remains the same size and stays in the same orientation.

Unit   Can have different meanings:
- an alternative word for ones in the place value of a number.
- the measurement name, e.g. km
- a unit fraction is any fraction that has a numerator of 1, e.g. $\frac{1}{5}$ or $\frac{1}{8}$

Vertex (plural: vertices)   The corner of a shape. In 2-D shapes, it is where two sides meet and in 3-D shapes it is where three or more edges meet.

Volume   The amount of space that a substance takes up inside a container.

English glossary

Adjective   A word used to modify nouns and proper nouns, e.g. colour, size or other features of an object or person.

Adverb   A word used to modify verbs (the way something is done), e.g. quietly, slowly, quickly, carefully. An adverb can also be used to modify an adjective, another adverb or a whole clause.

Adverbial of place   A word or phrase used to add further information about a place, e.g. in the swimming pool, beyond the mountains.

Adverbial of time   A word or phrase used to add further information about time, e.g. after the show, eventually.

Alliteration   The repetition of sounds in neighbouring or nearby words in a text, usually a consonant sound, e.g. caught carelessly creating a commotion.

Ambiguity   When something has more than one meaning.

Audience   Who a piece of writing is aimed at.

Brackets   Punctuation marks to show parenthesis in a text.

Character   A person (or thing with human qualities) who is part of a story or text.

Cohesion   When sentences and paragraphs flow into each other, making writing more organised, and easier to read and understand.

Comma   A punctuation mark used to separate items in a list, show different parts of a sentence, show parenthesis, and remove ambiguity.

Compound word   Words made from two or more other words, e.g. play + ground = playground, never + the + less = nevertheless.

Convention   A common feature or technique used by writers of different genres, e.g. good and evil characters in a fairytale.

Dash   A punctuation mark used to show a pause in a text. Also used in a pair to indicate parenthesis.

Definition   The meaning of a word.

Dictionary   A book containing an alphabetical list of words, with a definition of what each word means and what word class it is.

Editing   Making improvements to a piece of writing.

Embedded clause   A subordinate or relative clause within a main clause in a sentence.

Fact   Something that is true or real.

Figurative language   Words to suggest meaning by creating strong mental images for the reader.

Fronted adverbial   When the adverb or adverbial phrase occurs at the beginning of a sentence.

Homophone   Different words with different spellings that sound the same when spoken.

Hyphen   A punctuation mark sometimes used between a prefix and a root word.

Inference   Using ideas in a text to work out how or why something has happened, or how and why a character acts in or feels a certain way.

Infinitive   The basic form of a verb, e.g. to be, to go, to walk.

Intonation   The way words are spoken to enhance or emphasise their meaning.

Metaphor   Figurative language stating that something is something that it literally is not, e.g. 'a choir in the trees' referring to birds singing.

Modal verb   A word used to show how necessary or how possible something is, e.g. must, should, could, can, may, might, will

Near-homophone   Words which have different spellings and meanings but look and sound very similar.

Noun   The name of a person, place or thing.

Onomatopoeia   A word that sounds like the word's meaning, e.g. cuckoo, sizzle, pop.

Opinion   An idea held by at least one person but not necessarily by all.

Paragraph   A way of structuring text so sentences on the same topic are grouped together, e.g. one paragraph may include sentences describing a character and the next paragraph may include sentences about the setting.

Parenthesis   A word or phrase inserted into a text inside commas, brackets or dashes to give more information.

Personification   Figurative language giving human qualities to non-human objects.

Plan   The key ideas and sections a text will have. Notes written as part of a plan can then be used to help when writing the text.

Prediction   Thinking about what will happen next or later in a text, based on what has already been read.

Prefix   A letter/letters added to the beginning of a root word that change the word's meaning but not the spelling.

Proofreading   Reading through writing to check for sense and mistakes.

Purpose   The reason the text has been written.

Relative clause   A group of words used to add information about the noun in a sentence, which cannot stand alone as a sentence.

Relative pronoun   Used to link the noun to additional information in a relative clause, e.g. who, whose, which, that.

Retrieving   Finding information in a text to prove a point or to answer a question.

Root word   A word before any prefix or suffix is added to alter the meaning, e.g. jump (which can become jumper, jumped or jumping).

Setting   Where a story or poem takes place, i.e. where it is set.

Silent letter   A letter used in the spelling of the word which is not sounded when the word is spoken.

Simile   When two objects are compared using similar characteristics. Usually includes the word 'as' or 'like'. e.g. as cold as ice.

Subordinate clause   A subordinate clause is a clause that does not make sense without being attached to a main clause, e.g. before I went to school. It needs a main clause to make sense, e.g. I had breakfast before I went to school. Or: Before I went to school, I had breakfast.

Suffix   A letter/letters added to the end of a root word that change the word meaning.

Summarising   Picking out the main information from a text and briefly rewriting it in your own words.

Tense   When something happens – past, present or future.

Themes   Ideas put across by the author of a text, e.g. kindness, honesty, friendship, conflict.

Tone   The attitude with which words are meant or the expression of the voice to indicate feeling when said aloud.

Verb   Describes what the subject is 'doing', 'being' or 'having', e.g. She **reads** her book, **I am** tired, Zak **has** a new pen.

Volume   How loudly something is said.

Word class   How the word is used, e.g. an adjective, adverb, noun or verb.

Word ending   A letter/letters at the end of a word.

Word family   Groups of words that share similar spelling patterns or root words.

Acknowledgements

The authors and publisher are grateful to the copyright holders for permission to use quoted materials and images.
All images are ©Shutterstock.com and ©HarperCollins*Publishers*
Every effort has been made to trace copyright holders and obtain their permission for the use of copyright material. The authors and publisher will gladly receive information enabling them to rectify any error or omission in subsequent editions. All facts are correct at time of going to press.
Published by Collins
An imprint of HarperCollins*Publishers*
1 London Bridge Street
London SE1 9GF

HarperCollins*Publishers*
Macken House, 39/40 Mayor Street Upper,
Dublin 1, D01 C9W8, Ireland

ISBN: 978-0-00-839881-1
First published 2020
10 9 8 7 6 5
©HarperCollins*Publishers* Ltd. 2020

British Library Cataloguing in Publication Data.
A CIP record of this book is available from the British Library.
Authors: Jon Goulding and Tom Hall
Publisher: Fiona McGlade
Project Development: Katie Galloway
Cover Design: Kevin Robbins and Sarah Duxbury
Inside Concept Design: Ian Wrigley
Page Layout: Q2A Media
Production: Karen Nulty
Printed in the United Kingdom by Martins the Printers

MIX
Paper | Supporting responsible forestry
FSC™ C007454

This book contains FSC™ certified paper and other controlled sources to ensure responsible forest management.

For more information visit: www.harpercollins.co.uk/green

Progress charts

Use these charts to record your results in the six Progress Tests. Colour in the questions that you got right to help you identify any areas that you might need to study and practise again. (These areas are indicated in the 'See page…' row in the charts.)

Progress test 1: English

	Q1	Q2	Q3	Q4	Q5	Q6	Q7	Q8	Q9	Q10	Q11	Q12	Q13	TOTAL /57
See page…	4, 6	10	10	4, 6	12	18	6	14	4	14	10	10, 12	4, 6	

Progress test 2: Maths

	Q1	Q2	Q3	Q4	Q5	Q6	Q7	Q8	Q9	Q10	Q11	Q12	Q13	Q14	Q15	Q16	Q17	Q18	Q19	Q20	TOTAL /74
See page…	24	26	30	32	30	24	30, 38	30	32	26	28	26	30	24	26	34	32	30	26	34	
	Q21	Q22	Q23	Q24	Q25	Q26	Q27	Q28	Q29	Q30	Q31	Q32	Q33	Q34	Q35	Q36	Q37	Q38	Q39	Q40	
See page…	34, 38	34, 36	28	26	30	30, 38	26	32	34	28	30	30, 34	34	30	30, 28	34, 38	36	34	38	34	

Progress test 3: English

	Q1	Q2	Q3	Q4	Q5	Q6	Q7	Q8	Q9	Q10	Q11	Q12	Q13	TOTAL /55
See page…	44	10	52, 54	52	52	44	48	56	60	44	14	14	16	

Progress test 4: Maths

	Q1	Q2	Q3	Q4	Q5	Q6	Q7	Q8	Q9	Q10	Q11	Q12	Q13	Q14	Q15	Q16	Q17	Q18	Q19	TOTAL /71
See page…	24	26	30	30	34	72, 74	72, 74	78	80	84	24	24, 26	26	34, 38	32	28	36	76	80	
	Q20	Q21	Q22	Q23	Q24	Q25	Q26	Q27	Q28	Q29	Q30	Q31	Q32	Q33	Q34	Q35	Q36	Q37	Q38	
See page…	80, 82	28	34	34	68	72, 74, 78	84	30	32	82	32	38	70, 72, 74	70	84	86	78	82	38	

Progress test 5: English

	Q1	Q2	Q3	Q4	Q5	Q6	Q7	Q8	Q9	Q10	Q11	Q12	Q13	Q14	TOTAL /69
See page…	6	102	10	46	60, 62	92	94	96	104	10, 16	14	48	12, 10, 56	50	

Progress test 6: Maths

	Q1	Q2	Q3	Q4	Q5	Q6	Q7	Q8	Q9	Q10	Q11	Q12	Q13	TOTAL /43
See page…	30	110	110	80	38, 84	112	26	32	72, 74	84	114	34	38	
	Q14	Q15	Q16	Q17	Q18	Q19	Q20	Q21	Q22	Q23	Q24	Q25		
See page…	68	26	114	120	116	120	76	84	114	118	114	122		

Use this table to record your results for the Mixed questions sections on pages 128–143.

English mixed questions	Total score:	/ 106 marks
Maths mixed questions	Total score:	/ 126 marks